SHEM FLEENOR

RAMPARTS MAGAZINE'S RIGHTS REVOLUTION

1848 Publishing Company

New York City

ISBN: 9781951231-17-0

TABLE OF CONTENTS

INTRODUCTION

Page 4

CHAPTER ONE

"*Ramparts Magazine's* Revolutionary Rhetoric"

Page 12

CHAPTER TWO

"The Latino Rights Revolution"

Page 21

CHAPTER THREE

"Native Americans' Rights Revolution"

Page 52

CHAPTER FOUR

"African Americans' Rights Revolution"

Page 85

CHAPTER FIVE

"Women's Liberation"

Page 139

CHAPTER SIX

"America's Broken Healthcare System"
Page 225

CHAPTER SEVEN

"The Rise of the Modern Environmentalism"

Page 240

CHAPTER EIGHT

"The Counterculture"

Page 296

EPILOGUE

Page 389

INTRODUCTION

Ramparts Magazine, an American political muckraker that captured the revolutionary zeitgeist of the era, existed from 1962 – 1975. Unlike most of the radical magazines of its day, *Ramparts* was expensively produced and stylistically sophisticated. It was first established in June 1962 by Edward M. Keating in Menlo Park, California. It was originally intended to be a "showcase for the creative writer and as a forum for the mature American Catholic." The magazine declared its intent to publish fiction, poetry, art, criticism and essays of distinction, reflecting those "positive principles of the Hellenic-Christian tradition" that had "shaped and sustained western civilization for the previous two thousand years," and which were, Keating believed, still needed to "guide

American Catholics" in an age that had grown increasingly "secular, bewildered, and afraid."[1]

But under the editorship of Warren Hinckle, the look and ethos of *Ramparts* evolved, became a monthly news magazine, and moved its base of operation to San Francisco, California, which was an epicenter of the counterculture. Robert Scheer became managing editor and Dugald Stermer was hired as art director.[2] The trio proceeded to turn *Ramparts* into one of the best known and most respected organs of the American New Left.

The New Left can perhaps best be defined as a loosely organized and mostly white student movement that advocated democracy, civil rights, and various types of

---

[1] "Editorial Policy," *Ramparts*, vol. 1, no. 1 (June 1962), p. 3.

[2] Peter Richardson, *A Bomb in Every Issue: How the Short, Unruly Life of Ramparts Magazine Changed America*, (New York, The New Press, 2009).

university reforms. The proverbial tie that bound the disparate classes, races, nationalities, and ideas associated with the New Left was opposition to the American war in Indochina.

The term "New Left" was first popularized in the United States in an open letter written in 1960 by sociologist C. Wright Mills. It was titled *Letter to the New Left*. In it Mills argued for a new and improved leftist ideology that he hoped might transcend the traditional and often dogmatic "Old Left" focus on labor issues and subsequent lack of concern for issues such as racism, sexism, and the destruction of environment. Mills aimed to encourage a broader focus on issues such as opposing alienation, anomie, and authoritarianism. Mills thus argued for a shift from traditional leftism, toward the values of the counterculture, and, echoing Karl Marx, emphasized and advocated an international (rather than nationalistic) perspective on the movement. Mills also claimed that the proletariat (collectively the working-class referenced in Marxism) was no longer the revolutionary force in the postwar world; the new agents of revolutionary change in the decades after World War II were, Mills believed, young intellectuals such as college students, scholars, and editors of leftist academic books, journals, and muckraking publications.

Ramparts, perhaps more than any other American publication of the era, was especially committed to championing the values espoused by Mills. The magazine's editors were acutely attuned to and committed to social movements around the world. Many articles published in *Ramparts* thus either mentioned, explicitly focused on, or published essays contributed to the magazine by several inspirations, influences, key figures, and luminaries of the global New Left, including Mills, Albert Camus, Guy Debord, Simone de

Beauvoir, Allen Ginsberg, Emma Goldman, Che Guevara, Ho Chi Minh, Vladimir Lenin, Rosa Luxemburg, Herbert Marcuse, Bertrand Russell, Jean-Paul Sartre, Leon Trotsky, Malcolm X, Mao Zedong, Mahatma Gandhi, Stokely Carmichael, Noam Chomsky, Angela Davis, Régis Debray, Tom Hayden, Abbie Hoffman, Huey Newton, Carl Oglesby, Jerry Rubin, Mario Savio, Bobby Seale, Todd Gitlin, Howard Zinn, and César Chávez. The pages of *Ramparts,* in short, read like a who's who of the New Left.

Despite its profound cultural significance, by the time I began research on this series, only one book had been published about *Ramparts* – Peter Richardson's *A Bomb in Every Issue: How the Short, Unruly Life of Ramparts Magazine Changed America* (2009), which was awarded a *Mother Jones* Best Book of 2009 for its outstanding work uncovering the largely untold story of this great American muckraker. Richardson's book delved into the magazine's cultural significance and traced its trajectory from its 1962 birth as a "forum for the mature American Catholic" through its turbulent peak years (1967-1968), to its financially strapped demise in 1975. Richardson also deftly showed how *Ramparts* shaped the counterculture in the Bay Area of Northern California and vice versa. He also juxtaposed *Ramparts* against some of its contemporaries, most notably *Rolling Stone*, *Esquire*, and *Time*. Richardson also drew valuable connections to the later emergence of publications such as *Mother Jones*.

As great as *A Bomb in Every Issue* is as an examination of the external life and times of the magazine and the middle-class white men at helm of *Ramparts*, I was, as a historian with a background in journalism, more interested in the inner-life of the magazine and the publication's depiction and coverage of many of the most seminal events in both American and world history during the 1960s and early

1970s. In other words, I was more interested in the magazine as journalistic history and the magazine's incredible primary source material.

By the time I began research on this series, *Ramparts* had been fully digitized online. The digital archive spanned thirteen of the most turbulent years in world history. It thus provides an invaluable database of primary source material with which to get a great sense of how the American New Left narrated the events that shaped the Vietnam era in American history, including the rise and demise of the New Left as a viable political force in the American polity.

The database offers readers a window into an America in which leftism was actually a viable political alternative and force that seemed to have a profound impact on the nation's culture and political system. By September 11, 2001, there was no viable antiwar movement or rights revolution that was even remotely comparable to the movements unabashedly championed in the pages of *Ramparts*. By the turn of the twenty-first century, both major political parties in the United States were unwavering proponents of American militarism as the cornerstone institution in American life, and neither the Democratic or Republican political parties had programs designed to address the same inveterate racism, sexism, poverty, and degradation of the environment that were routinely addressed in the pages of *Ramparts* in the late-1960 and early 1970s. The militarism, corruption, warfare, and corporate welfare that *Ramparts* routinely exposed had not, in short, significantly abated in the decades after the end of the Vietnam War; in many cases the economic and political corruption that Ramparts sought to expose was far worse at the turn of the twenty-first century than in 1975, when the final issue of *Ramparts* was published.

This book is titled *Ramparts Magazine's Rights Revolution*. It provides an examination of the muckraking publication's unabashed championing of the courageous efforts of traditionally marginalized Americans demanding civil rights and social equality. The chapters focus specifically on Mexican American, Native American, and African American efforts to attain economic and political equality. Those chapters are followed by essays focused on the publication's coverage of the Women's Liberation Movement; the notion that all Americans had a right to adequate and affordable healthcare; the rise of the Modern Environmentalist Movement; and the growing prominence of what came to be known as the counterculture in American society during the 1960s and 1970s.

CHAPTER ONE

"*Ramparts Magazine's* Revolutionary Rhetoric"

Ramparts Magazine was both a product and purveyor of a revolutionary age. But the magazine likewise advocated revolution. The editors of the magazine were deeply dedicated to exposing inveterate corruption in the American economic, legal, and political system. The editors also unabashedly championed revolutionary movements on every continent sans Antarctica, including the Black Panthers, who were Bay Area neighbors and fellow travelers with the editorial staff at *Ramparts*. Eldridge Cleaver, in fact, became a writer for *Ramparts* after his release from prison, then only later became a member of the Black Panther Party. Numerous stories published by the magazine were, in short, advocation for revolution and/or revolutionaries.

The first such article published by *Ramparts* was an essay titled "John Quincy Adams and the Revolutionary Temper," written by novelist Truman Nelson. Nelson's essay about Adams was followed immediately in the December 1964 edition of *Ramparts* by profile of Mahatmas Gandhi, written by the Christian mystic Thomas Merton, who, like Martin Luther King Jr., believed the world desperately needed a moral revolution. In a way, Merton humanized anti-colonialism for a Catholic-American audience via his celebration of Gandhi by writing that the latter "believed that the central problem of our time was the acceptance or the rejection of a basic law of love and of truth which had been made known to the world in traditional religions and most clearly by Jesus Christ." Gandhi himself, Merton wrote, "expressly and very clearly declared himself an adherent of this one law" and was "indisputably sincere and right in his moral commitment to the law of love and truth."[3]

---

[3] Thomas Merton, "The Gentle Revolutionary," *Ramparts Magazine*, December 1964, p. 30.

In May 1965, *Ramparts* published an opinion piece titled "The Triple Revolution," contributed by W.H. Ferry, who was a director of The Center for the Study of Democratic Institutions in Santa Barbara, California. He declared that a "moral equivalent to war" was a requisite part of waging what he referred to as a "triple revolution" that he imagined might transform mankind from what he called "homoeconimicus" to "homohumanus." In other words, Ferry proscribed that a human rights revolution in which humans were motivated by love and care for each other rather than motivated by accruing more wealth and material comfort as fast as possible was especially requisite, lest humanity would soon self-destruct.

In October 1965, *Ramparts* published Robert McAfee Brown's address to the parents of Stanford University's Class of 1965 titled, "This Revolting Generation." In it Brown lamented that many adults, including the longtime director of Federal Bureau of Investigation, J. Edgar Hoover, denigrated the 1964-65 manifestations of student unrest on American campuses, most notably the University of California at Berkeley, as a product of immaturity and insecurity, and believed it to be evidence of an association of American college kids with the more dubious members of the faculty, or (in an increasingly widespread variant) to some kind of Communist takeover of the student organizations. Brown expressed regret that Hoover seemed "more concerned about exposing purported Communist activity in Berkeley than in exposing manifest, blatant Fascist activity in Mississippi."[4] Brown thus also considered the young generation to be "revolting" but he meant it in the best possible sense; as in revolting against the staid fascism

---

[4] Robert McAfee Brown, "This Revolting Generation," *Ramparts Magazine*, October 1965, p. 14.

in American society as personified by J. Edgar Hoover.

Even the Roman Catholic Church seemed to be in the midst of a social and cultural revolution in the 1960s. *Ramparts* editor Warren Hinkle thus continued the theme of radical religious activism common in the magazine in the November 1967 edition in an article titled "Left Wing Catholics." Though the American clergy depicted by Hinckle was by no means as militant or revolutionary as Father Camilo Torre, there was, Hinckle asserted, a liberalization of the Church happening all over the world, not just in Latin America. The Church had often supported the anti-Semitism and snarling fascism in Europe in the interwar era and emerged from World War II with a diminished moral authority and thus diminished cultural influence, which, in part, led to the Second Vatican Council, which lasted from 1962 – 1965/ Vatican II, some scholars believe, is evidence of the liberalization of the Church as it tried to maintain some semblance of cultural importance in the context of modern revolutionary movements evolving throughout the developing world.

In the United States, the Church was by no means a radical institution, but it also was not free from being affected by anti-colonialism. Fulton Sheen of Rochester, New York, who Hinckle referred to as "the great, gray eminence of the early days of televangelism, who stood up in his pulpit every Sunday night against Milton Berle and Ed Sullivan," held a captive audience in the 1950s with theatrical lectures on the deadly menace of communism and the "real dangers of atheistic materialism," had, by 1967, suddenly advocated the U.S. withdrawing from Vietnam. Sheen, Hinckle believed, had grown so concerned over the Church's deafening silence on Vietnam that he publicly beseeched President Lyndon Johnson to "immediately" withdraw U.S. all forces. Suddenly, Sheen was," Hinckle wrote, "Paul and Rochester was Damascus... It was a conversion. A miracle."[5]

Other case studies of American Catholic priests advocating liberalism included James Groppi of Milwaukee, Wisconsin, who said to the Youth Council of the Milwaukee NAACP that "Jesus Christ was the greatest civil rights worker."[6] Hinkle concluded by delving into Pope Paul VI's seeming radical turn in the 1960s. Hinckle cited Pope Paul VI's *Populorum Progressio* (*On the Development of Peoples*), which was called "warmed-over Marxism" and dismissed by *Fortune Magazine* as taking a "dated stand and suspicious view of the workings of capitalist economic enterprise."[7]

---

[5] Warren Hinckle, "Left Wing Catholics," *Ramparts Magazine*, November 1967, p. 23

[6] Ibid, p. 19.

[7] Ibid, p. 26.

In May 1969, *Ramparts* published a spoof contributed by Mary Morhoff of Parker Brother's popular boardgame Monopoly, which she described as capitalism for kids. Morhoff's centerfold and set of rules was meant to be the antithesis of Monopoly – a boardgame title "Revolution." The spoof seemed meant to underscore how entrenched and naturalized the spirit of winner-take-all capitalism was entrenched in American society in the late 1960s, so much so that kids divided and conquered each other for fun.

Ramparts was, as the pages that follow illuminate, a voice of what seemed poised to be a revolutionary epoch in American history. The magazine's editors were dedicated to championing a true rights revolution that would transform American society via its institutions. The editors, as the following chapter illuminate, published several articles about the American Labor movement, African Americans, Mexican Americans, and Native

Americans' quest for political and economic equality. The later essays in this book focus on *Ramparts Magazine's* championing women's liberation. Several stories published in *Ramparts* also, as later chapters highlight, defended readers' rights to live in a safe and healthy environment. Environmentalism, in fact, evolved out of the counterculture, which was a general movement of people dedicated to living lives conscientiously removed from the rapaciousness, greed, and destruction part and parcel of Cold War American capitalism.

CHAPTER TWO

"The Latino Rights Revolution"

Ramparts Magazine published several stories championing the Latino rights revolution, particularly the Chicano Movement. In September 1965, for example, *Ramparts* published a two-part special report titled "Bracero Politics." The first essay in the series was titled "No Dice for Braceros," contributed by William Turner, an ex-FBI agent who was an expert on scientific methods of crime detection. Though the *de jure* Bracero Program that had existed since World War II was ended by the federal government in 1964, Turner found that it was *de facto* in California. Since the Bracero Program ensured a constant supply of cheap immigrant labor for growers, immigrants could not protest any infringement of their basic human rights, lest they be fired and replaced.

Turner's essay chronicled how California agri-business had grown too big to fail in the decades after World War II. The bigger California's agri-business grew, Turner asserted, the more dire social conditions became for farm laborers who worked these industrial farms, many of whom were of Mexican ancestry. Turner also underscored the political power of agri-business in a state that fed forty percent of the nation. The power of agri-business was in stark contrast to the lack of socioeconomic power of what he referred to as a captive labor force that was dependent on meager wages for subsistence living. Cesar Chavez and Delores Huerta of the United Farm Workers, were, Turner explained, at the forefront of a fevered battle against the Bracero Program. Their opposition stemmed from their belief that the program undermined American workers and concomitantly exploited the migrant workers to the obscene benefit of the managers. Chavez's and Huerta's efforts contributed to Congress finally ending the *de jure* Bracero Program in 1964. But a de facto Bracero system continues all through the American southwest in the twenty-first century.

Also in September 1965, *Ramparts* published an essay written by John Beecher, who was a former chief of the Farm Security Administration in Florida. His essay was titled "To the Rear, March! 1965-1940," which included photos contributed by Ernest Lowe.

The Farm Security Administration was a New Deal agency within the United States Department of Agriculture. It had developed in the areas of migrant concentration, a program (long since scuttled) of model camps, small homes, clinics, community centers and even hospitals for migratory workers. Beecher had previously made field studies of the migrant problem in California, Arizona, and Texas, Florida, and other parts of the eastern U.S. He was thus called to testify in May and August 1940, before two Congressional Committees which were drafting a study of migrancy – the famous La Follette Committee or Senate Committee on Civil Liberties – and also the Select Committee to Investigate the Interstate Migration of Destitute Citizens, known as the Tolan Committee.

Beecher's *Ramparts* essay consisted of excerpts from his 25-year-old testimony given before these two Congressional Committees. The photographs and the text depicted the situation in 1965 in a typical migrant areas. Together, his testimony and the images made plain that there had been no significant reform since the 1940s in these migrant communities. In some instances, in places like Pahokee, Florida, the situation had grown far more dire since he first testified to Congress. For example, in Palm Beach County, which was per capita one of the wealthiest in the U.S., the mostly African American and Bahamian farm workers were some of the most indigent in the nation, suffering conditions comparable to Third World nations in terms of starvation, lack of medical care, and access to quality education. Beecher concluded by noting the desperate importance of farm workers in Palm Beach County organizing themselves much as the United Farm Workers had in California's San Joaquin Valley.

In July 1966, *Ramparts* published a four-part series titled "Tales of the Delano Revolution." The first essay in the series was an editorial written by Paul Jacobs. It was accompanied with quaint John Kouns photos taken of Cesar Chavez and other members of the UFW, which was stylistically reminiscent of a Norman Rockwell painting. Jacobs' essay chronicled a recent 300-mile march from Delano, California to the state's capital, Sacramento. Jacobs referred to congregation of marchers as "a class reunion of liberals, radicals, and ex-radicals." Even old animosities, political and personal, he added, "were submerged, if not forgotten, in the genuine joy" the marchers "felt at what was happening on the steps" of the capital building. The congregation, Jacobs explained, joined in jeering the name of Governor Pat Brown, who had refused to meet with the marchers that day, preferring to spend it with his family at Frank Sinatra's home in Palm Springs.[8]

---

[8] Paul Jacobs, "Tales of the Delano Revolution," *Ramparts Magazine*, July 1966, p. 37.

Jacobs further elaborated the historical context of the events by explaining thirty years of failed attempts to organize such a cohesive moment due to the farm workers themselves not leading the movement until recent years when the likes of Huerta and Chavez took a more direct and activist role in the movement, which seemed, to Jacobs, to make all the difference. The pilgrimage from Delano grew out of a tough strike against the grape growers of Kern and Tulare counties, begun in September of 1966 by the Agricultural Workers Organizing Committee, but led by Chavez and the National Farm Workers Association. These labor unions launched a nationwide boycott of Schenley Products, and when Schenley agreed to sign a collective bargaining contract with the NFWA, they followed with a boycott of the products of DiGiorgio, the largest grower in the strike zone. Hundreds of groups and millions of individuals all over the country provided assistance in the boycott, but the operation was, Jacobs noted, always run by the NFWA. "It was," he explained, "a new kind of farm strike, a new kind of farm labor movement, which put the campesinos in the driver's seat." It was, Jacobs concluded, "the source of new hope that these most exploited of American workers may one day enjoy the fruits of their labor."[9]

The second essay in the "Tales of the Delano Revolution" published by *Ramparts* in July 1966 was titled "The Tale of The Raza," written by Luis Valdez. He explained that La Raza (the race) was the Mexican people and referred to it as "sentimental and cynical, fierce and docile, faithful and treacherous, individualistic and herd-following, in love with life and obsessed with death." The personality of la Raza also, he added, "encompassed all the complexity of our

---

[9] Ibid, p. 37.

history... Below the foundations of our Spanish culture, we still sense the ruins of an entirely different civilization."[10]

Valdez acknowledged the fact that so many Mexicans spoke of themselves as a "race" was a massive contradiction because, he explained, the conquistadores had mated with Indian women with "customary abandon," creating a "nation of bewildered half-breeds in countless shapes, colors and sizes." But these mestizos, he proudly declared, solved the problem with poetic license and called themselves La Raza. At best, he added, La Raza's "cultural schizophrenia" had led many to action through the all-encompassing poetry of religion, which was "a fancy way of saying blind faith." The Virgin of Guadalupe, the supreme poetic expression of Mexican desire to be one people, had, he noted, inspired Mexicans more than once to social revolution.

---

[10] Luis Valdez, "The Tale of La Raza," *Ramparts Magazine*, July 1966, p. 40.

At worst, Valdez wrote, the two-sidedness of being Mexican had traditionally led to inaction. The last divine Aztec emperor Cuauhtémoc, Valdez rued, was murdered in the jungles of Guatemala, and his descendants were put to work in the fields. "We are still there," he lamented, "in dry, plain, American Delano." But the triple magnetism of Raza, patria, and the Virgin of Guadalupe which organized the Mexican-American farm worker in Delano — that and Cesar Chavez had helped Mexicans reconcile the dilemma, which paved the way for substantive social activism. Chavez was not a traditional bombastic Mexican revolutionary, Valdez explained. Nor was he a gavacho, a gringo, a white social worker type. Both types had tried to organize La Raza in America and had failed. Cesar was, however, Valdez hailed, "our first real Mexican-American leader."[11]

---

[11] Ibid, p. 40.

The third essay in the "Tales of the Delano Revolution" series was titled "The Nun's Tale." It was contributed by Sister Mary Prudence, who was a teacher at Guadalupe College in Los Gatos, California. She described the 300-mile odyssey from Delano to Sacramento. In spite of physical hardship and police harassment she was inspired by the justice of their movement and the marchers' "Christ-like spirit." She explained that on the arduous march to the capital building she had finally learned what it meant to "be a minority."[12] She noted that many of the farm owners who were adversarial to the marchers were also devoutly Catholic. One of them said to her "Sister, you are ruining the image of the Church." She scoffed notion. "And what about the Gospel of the Church?" she replied to the farm owner. "And what about the duties of the Church, to God's people? Together," she

---

[12] Sister Mary Prudence, "A Nun's Tale," *Ramparts Magazine*, July 1966, p. 43.

declared, "we (the marchers) manifest the brotherhood of man."[13]

The first three essays all paid homage to Chavez as being a leader cut from the same cloth as Christ the Messiah. The final essay contributed to the series was written by Chavez himself. It was titled "The Organizer's Tale." Chavez explained the difficulty of the strike, writing, "I went through a lot of hell, and a lot of people did," but, he added, "if we can even the score a little for the workers then we are doing something."[14] In 1962, Chavez co-founded the NFWA with Huerta. When Filipino American farm workers initiated the Delano grape strike on September 8, 1965, to protest for higher wages, Chavez openly supported them. Six months later, he and the NFWA led a strike of California grape pickers on the march from Delano to Sacramento

---

[13] Ibid, p. 43.

[14] Cesar Chavez, "The Organizer's Tale," *Ramparts Magazine*, July 1966, p. 50.

demanding similar concessions. The renamed United Farm Workers (UFW) encouraged all Americans to boycott table grapes as a show of solidarity with the striking farmers who were demanding basic human rights.

The strike endured for five years and attracted worldwide attention. Chavez eventually received support from labor leader Walter Reuther who, in December 1965, marched with the striking grape pickers in Delano. Reuther's support made it more difficult for the grape growers to ignore the strikers. During his visit, Reuther pledged to provide $7,500 per month to the farm workers' strike fund for the duration of the walkout. In March 1966, the U.S. Supreme Court Committee on Labor and Public Welfare's Subcommittee on Migratory Labor held hearings in California on the strike. During the hearings, subcommittee member Robert F. Kennedy openly expressed his support for the striking workers. The UFW during Chavez's tenure was also committed to restricting import of immigrant labor.

In September 1970, *Ramparts* published an essay titled "Ford and La Raza," written by Rees Lloyd and Peter Montague, who were free-lance writers living in New Mexico who were associated with *El Grito del Norte*, a bilingual newspaper. Lloyd and Montague wrote that in 1846 the U.S. Army had invaded New Mexico. But by 1970 the state had been invaded again by the Ford Foundation. The intent of both invasions was, they sardonically argued, the same as it has always been: "to 'benefit' the natives" — this time with a "pacification program" aimed at heading off the new militancy of Native Americans and Mexican Americans, creating a "poverty-foundation complex, and building up a 'safe' leadership for La Raza akin to the NAACP or the Urban League."15

Ford's single largest investment had been a $1.5 million loan to establish a huge cattle feedlot in La Jara, Colorado. The model of Ford's "constructive direction," the essayists lamented, was the multimillion dollar cattle feedlot which Ford set up in La Jara, Colorado, with satellite feedlots to be built in northern New Mexico. The feedlot sprawled across two-hundred acres, with a hundred and twenty feeding pens capable of accommodating 15,000 cattle. It contained an ultra-sophisticated push-button feed-mixing mill, whose superstructure and three large silos rose before the gleaming new offices which Ford had built for the management, headed by Claude Lowry, an Anglo cattle trader from New Mexico, who the essayists described as a jingoistic colonial

---

15 Rees Lloyd and Peter Montague, "Ford and La Raza," *Ramparts Magazine*, September 1970, p. 10.

overlord whose primary goal was to enrich the Ford Foundation at the expense of indigent Mexican Americans in northern New Mexico, most of whom were making minimum wage to serve the interests of agricultural corporations associated with Ford Foundation brass. After this multi-million dollar business was created, Lloyd and Montague explained, it was surreptitiously handed over to the brother-in-law of the same Ford executive who had publicly announced the feedlot as an example of the Foundation's supposed bounty. "This is a major scandal that has been covered up," the essayists wrote.[16] And as a result of the scandal, the Anglo benefactors received good publicity, while the workers got subsistence wages.

Lloyd and Montague also interviewed Jose Madril, who had taken part in the armed raid on Tierra Amarilla Court House in June of

---

[16] Ibid, p. 10.

1967 in the hopes making a citizen's arrest on district attorney, Alfonso Sanchez. A state patrolman and the jailer were shot and seriously wounded. Two others, a reporter and a deputy sheriff, were held captive all afternoon on the New Mexico countryside, which led to the largest manhunt in New Mexico history. The two hostages were soon released and Reies Tijerina, the founder of La Alianza Federal de Mercedes (Federal Alliance of Land Grants), was soon captured, tried and convicted of assault. Because of that, he received a two-year prison sentence. At a time when Mexican Americans were often called "the sleeping giant," the hostility of Tijerina's shoot-out, Lloyd and Montague argued, inspired a whole generation of young Chicanos who suddenly saw that it was possible to protest the injustices they often endured. Lloyd and Montague thus saw the Ford Foundation as a counterrevolutionary force sent to occupy and pacify what they perceived to be a budding rebellion.

In March 1971, *Ramparts* published an essay titled "Los Siete de la Raza," contributed by Marjorie Heins, who was a free-lance journalist living in San Francisco, California. Her story chronicled Los Siete de la Raza, the name the media had given to seven young Latinos named Gary Lescallett, Rodolfo Antonio (Tony) Martinez, Mario Martinez, Jose Rios, Nelson Rodriguez, and Danilo Melendez. These men were from the Mission District of San Francisco. They were, she explained, involved in an altercation with the police that resulted in the death of an officer in 1969.

The young Latinos included four Salvadorans, one Nicaraguan, and one Honduran, some of whom had been involved in a youth group dubbed the Mission Rebels (founded in 1965), and later in pan-Latino organizations such as COBRA (Confederation of Brown Race for Action) at the College of San Mateo, and the Brown Berets. The young men were approached by Joe Brodnik and Paul McGoran, two plainclothes SFPD officers, while moving a stereo or TV into a house on May 1, 1969 at around 10:30 a.m. A struggle ensued and Brodnik was fatally shot with his partner's pistol.

The incident and the subsequent trial became a cause célèbre of the Latin-American community and the New Left. The trial began in June 1970 and the court sessions were widely attended by young radicals, including Huey Newton, and members of the Chicago Seven. The accused argued that McGoran had pulled his gun and shot Brodnik during his struggle with one of the defendants. McGoran and the prosecution argued that he did not remove his gun from his holster and that all he could remember was being attacked. His estranged wife gave testimony during the trial that her husband would sometimes carry marijuana and other drugs on him that he would plant on suspects to ensure their conviction. The essay concluded by soliciting funds for the defense. Los Siete de la Raza were ultimately acquitted of Brodnik's murder.

In November 1972, *Ramparts* published an essay titled "La Raza Unida Comes Together," contributed by Rodrigo Reyes, who was a free-lance journalist who had also been working on "Reflecciones de la Raza," a news program on *KPFA-FM*, in Berkeley, California. The article chronicled the founding and some of the founders of La Raza Unida Party (LARUP), which was a political party centered on Chicano nationalism. It was born in the early 1970s and became prominent throughout Texas and Southern California. It was started to combat growing inequality and dissatisfaction with the Democratic Party, which was typically supported by Mexican-American voters. After its establishment in Texas, the party launched electoral campaigns in Colorado, Arizona, New Mexico, and California, though it only secured official party status for statewide races in Texas. Although La Raza Unida supported the struggle of United Farm Workers, it strongly disagreed with the endorsement of Senator George McGovern by UFWOC's leadership, most notably Cesar Chavez. La Raza Unida's platform included measures which called for:

> Support for neither of two major party candidates for President of the United States.
>
> Support for the right to strike and support of the Farm Workers Union.
>
> An immediate withdrawal of troops from Vietnam and Indochina; guaranteed annual income.
>
> Responsible support to La Raza women in their struggle for equal rights in all spheres of life; Chicano community control of law enforcement agencies.

elimination of U.S. economic and military intervention in Latin America.

Support for Puerto Rican Independence; an end to exploitation of illegal aliens;

Government subsidies to be shared with laborers who worked for subsidized farmers.

An end of right-to-work laws; redistribution of wealth and the break-up of monopolies.

Bi-lingual and bi-cultural education for La Raza throughout the education system.

Increased opportunities for Chicanos in higher education to have greater representation in the professions.

Adequate housing.

Free clinics.

An end to drug traffic in Chicano communities; active support of prison reform.

Free legal aid to insure adequate legal representation for La Raza.

Chicanos to serve in judgeships and juries at all levels.

Enforcement of the treaty of Guadalupe Hidalgo.

Honor of original Mexican and Spanish land grants.

Community control of social, economic and political institutions — Chicano self-determination.[17]

In August 1973, *Ramparts* published a report titled "Chavez and the Teamsters: Showdown in the Coachella Valley,"

---

[17] Rodrigo Reyes, "La Raza Unida Comes Together," *Ramparts Magazine*, November 1972, p. 24.

contributed by George Baker, who was a San Joaquin Valley newsman who had been following the farm labor scene for many years. Baker's essay chronicled a recent deadly clash between the International Brotherhood of Teamsters and UFW picketers, and delved into a deeper history of conflict that had festered between the two unions. In 1970, Baker explained, Chavez decided to move the UFW's headquarters from Delano to La Paz, California, where he hoped to transform the organization into an entity dedicated to serving the needs of all who suffered.

Other union members, however, objected to this distancing of the leadership away from the farm workers' movement. The union was poised to launch its next major campaign in the lettuce fields in 1970. The Teamsters initially signed contracts with lettuce growers in the Salinas Valley, because the union wanted to avoid recognizing the UFW. Then in 1973, when the three-year UFW grape contracts expired, the grape growers signed contracts giving the Teamsters the right to represent the workers who had been members of the UFW. The UFW responded with strikes, lawsuits and boycotts, including secondary boycotts in the retail grocery industry. The UFW, however, struggled to regain the members that had defected and it never fully recovered its strength. The battles in the fields became violent. Some UFW members were killed on the picket line. The violence led the state of California to in 1975 enact the California Agricultural Labor Relations Act, creating an administrative agency to oversee secret ballot elections and to resolve charges of unfair labor practices, like failing to bargain in good faith, or discrimination against activists.

In December 1974, *Ramparts* published a second essay written by Baker titled "The Teamster Raid: Stalled in the Vineyards." The Teamsters and UFW had both claimed jurisdiction over farm workers for many years, and in 1967 had signed an agreement to settle their differences. But decentralization of power within the union led several Teamster leaders in California to, without General President Frank Fitzsimmons' permission, repudiate this agreement and organize large numbers of field workers. His hand forced, Fitzsimmons ordered Teamsters contract negotiators to re-open the handful of contracts it had signed with California growers.

The UFW sued, the AFL-CIO condemned the action, and many employers negotiated contracts with the Teamsters rather than with the UFW. The Teamsters subsequently signed contracts (which many denounced as sweetheart deals) with almost four hundred California growers. Although an agreement giving UFW jurisdiction over field workers and the Teamsters' jurisdiction over packing and warehouse workers was reached on September 27, 1973, Fitzsimmons reneged on the agreement within a month and moved ahead with forming a farm workers regional union in California.

By 1975, the UFW had won twenty-four elections through secret ballots and the Teamsters only fourteen. By then, however, UFW membership had plummeted to just 6,000 from nearly 70,000 concomitant to the Teamsters farm worker division growing to 55,000 workers. The UFW signed an agreement with Fitzsimmons in March 1977 in which the UFW agreed to seek to organize only those workers covered by the California Agricultural Labor Relations Act, while the Teamsters retained jurisdiction over some agricultural workers, who had been covered by Teamsters Local Union contracts prior to the formation of the UFW.

"The Teamster Raid: Stalled in the Vineyards" was followed in the December 1974 edition of *Ramparts* by an essay titled "Can

Chavez Win?" The essay was contributed by Rick Beban, who was an editor for *The Pacific Sun*. In it Beban argued that the fate of UFW and the dwindling numbers of farm workers they represented hinged on the election of Edmund "Jerry" Brown as governor. With Brown on his way to the governor's mansion, the UFW planned to reintroduce legislation that was narrowly defeated in California's previous legislative session, which would give farm workers the right to supervised free elections but would not take away the right to secondary boycotts. The growers had maintained that they would have liked free elections under the National Labor Relations Act, but the UFW had resisted inclusion of farm workers because the NLRA prohibited secondary boycotts, thereby diminishing the organization's ability to organize and collectively bargain. The farm worker bill would have paralleled the NLRA, but without what the UFW felt were its restrictive provisions. With Brown in the governor's mansion and a new, Democratic legislature, UFW leadership believed it could pass the kind of bill they had been pushing for, hold elections in the fields, and thus chase the Teamsters out of California.

In April 1975, *Ramparts* published a photo essay titled "The UFW: A Moment of Rebirth," contributed by Daniel Hunter and Diane Coleman about a recent march of 10,000 sympathizers of the UFW, led by Cesar Chavez, in Modesto, California. As marchers streamed through this city of 85,000 residents where the giant E&J Gallo winery, the nation's largest, was headquartered, they chanted bilingual slogans such as: "Boycott Gallo" and "Viva la Huelga."

The march was part of an effort to compel the fully industrialized winery to let the farm workers vote for whom they wanted to represent them – the UFW or the Teamsters.

Chavez was confident that a vote via secret ballot would show that the farm workers overwhelmingly wanted to be represented by the UFW. As the title of the essay indicated, there seemed to be great optimism that the UFW, whose membership had been in sharp decline all through the early 1970s, was regaining its strength and political viability. Indeed in 1977, the Teamsters finally signed an agreement with the UFW promising to end their efforts to represent farm workers. But in the late 1970s, the leadership of the UFW was wracked by a series of conflicts, as differences emerged between Chavez and some of his former colleagues about what direction the organization should take, what interests the organization should champion, and whether the organization should be more locally or globally focused.

In 1977, Chavez met with then-President of the Philippines Ferdinand Marcos in Manila and endorsed his regime, which was seen by many human rights advocates and religious leaders as a ruthless and oppressive dictatorship. Phillip Vera Cruz resigned from the UFW in protest of Chavez's support of Marcos. Chavez also clashed with several UFW members about policy issues, including the proposed creation of local unions for the UFW, which was typical for national unions. Chavez, however, adamantly opposed local control on the grounds that it detracted from his vision for the UFW as a social movement global in scope and vision. By the end of the 1970s, only one member of the UFW's original board of directors remained. Still, before the turn of the 1980s, Chavez's tactics had forced growers to recognize the UFW as the bargaining agent for 50,000 field workers in California and Florida. In 1988, at the tail end of the second Reagan administration, Chavez attempted another grape boycott to protest the exposure of farm workers to dangerous pesticides. The boycott, however, failed, which seemed a metaphor for how drastically the nation had become removed from the social activism that defined American society in the 1960s and early 1970s.

CHAPTER THREE

"Native Americans' Rights Revolution"

Ramparts Magazine published some groundbreaking stories about the historical oppression of Native Americans and American Indians attempts to redress the fact that full citizenship had been systemically denied to them by the white power structure in United States since the nation was founded. The first such article that *Ramparts* published that specifically addressed Native Americans quest for civil rights was published in the summer of 1964. The essay was titled "The Morality of Indian Hating." It was contributed by N. Scott Momaday, who taught in the English Department at the University of California at Santa Barbara. In it he addressed the

Relocation Program, which he described as the most recent attempt by the Bureau of Indian Affairs to accelerate integration of Native Americans into the hegemonic white urban-industrial society.

At a time when the U.S. government was decreasing subsidies to Indians living on reservations, the Relocation Act offered to pay moving expenses and provide some vocational training for those who were willing to move from the reservations to certain government-designated cities, where employment opportunities were thought to be more favorable. Types of assistance included relocation transportation, transportation of household goods, subsistence per diem for both the time of relocation and up to four weeks after arrival, and funds to purchase tools or equipment for apprentice workers. Additional benefits included: medical insurance for workers and their dependents, grants to purchase work clothing, grants to purchase household goods and furniture, tuition costs for vocational night-school training, and in some cases funds to help purchase a home.

The rewards of urban civilization, however, as Momaday noted, could not compensate for the loss of tribal identity, and more than twenty percent of the relocated Indians returned disenchanted to the reservations. Like allotment in previous generations, relocation was, Momaday believed, attractive on paper but less desirable in practice. If an Indian consented to be relocated, he explained, his transportation expenses were to be paid by the government; he was also provided with employment and lodging. He had access to recreational and counseling facilities, and was also entitled to the services of specially-trained social workers.

But the failure of relocation, Momaday underscored, resided with the premise upon which it was based: that the Indian "became a white man by virtue of living in the presence of white men." The Indian in the city was, Momaday lamented, "victimized by the very things which defined urban existence." The American Indian could neither understand nor be understood because his knowledge of English was inadequate," Momaday explained. The American Indian lured to cities by government incentives also "could not support himself or his family because he knew nothing of urban economics." Worst of all, Momaday added, Native Americans lured from tribal lands to cities could not "clear his mind of the innumerable doubts and fears" which an "alien civilization imposed upon him" because he was an Indian. "None but an Indian," Momaday wrote, "knows so well what it is like to have incomplete existence in two worlds and security in neither."

Relocation was also, he noted, flagrantly misrepresented to the Indian considering that the accommodations he was provided by the government were often sub-standard. He argued that despite being championed as high-minded white morality, that relocation was in practice guided not by morality but by economics. The infamous Termination Bills – Congressional legislation designed to terminate federal responsibility for Indians at the earliest possible date – had, Momaday believed, "greatly retarded" the process of acculturation and invited exploitation of Indian property. The responsibility for Indian education and development of Indian land resources was also gradually turned over from federal authority to state jurisdiction during the postwar era.[18]

In March 1967, *Ramparts* published an essay contributed by David Welch titled "The Passamaquoddy Indians." The

---

[18] N. Scott Momaday, "The Morality of Indian Hating," *Ramparts Magazine*, Summer 1964, p. 38.

Passamaquoddy are an American Indian/First Nations people who originally lived in northeastern North America, primarily in Maine and New Brunswick, Canada. In 1967, the nation filed a land claim demanding land they believed that had a legal right to own. They argued that the tribe's rights under a critical 1794 treaty, including ownership of a trust fund and vast tracts of subsequently stolen land, had been violated.

Outside of the tribe, Welch explained, the treaty had been entirely forgotten. The Indians themselves had only discovered the treaty in 1962. The treaty had been originally negotiated in 1794 with the state of Massachusetts, which controlled Maine at the time, and under it the Passamaquoddy had surrendered their ancestral lands in exchange for perpetual ownership of fifteen islands in the St. Croix River, two in Big Lake, ten acres at Pleasant Point, and the entirety of what came to be called Indian Township, which was

23,000 acres of forest, streams and lakes in what would later be eastern Washington County that the tribe had used as winter hunting grounds since time immemorial. Recognizing the Indians would not be able to sustain themselves entirely on this reduced land base, they were also given a trust fund – $37,471 in 1822, or $147 million if it had just been left to compound interest through 1964.

When Maine became a state in 1820, it received this trust fund and 395,000 acres of deeded land meant to provide for the Indians. Under the separation agreement with Massachusetts, not only was Maine required to uphold the 1794 treaty obligations, but they were written into the new state's constitution. But rather than protecting the Indians' trust lands, the state authorized some tracts to be flooded by dams, others to be annexed for the laying out of Route-1 in Indian Township and Route-190 at Pleasant Point, and thousands more acres transferred to white owners. In no

58

case was compensation given to the Indians. In all, at least 10,000 acres had been stolen, among them the small plot where a gravel pile protest had taken place in 1964.

Maine courts had ignored the tribe's treaty rights, rubber-stamping the annexation of their lands by powerful landowners such as William Bingham (for whom the mountain is named) and, in the infamous 1892 case of *State vs. Newell*, ruling the tribe no longer existed. As for the 1794 treaty, it had long been forgotten, and in 1964 state officials were publicly dismissing its validity. Privately, however, Governor John Reed's administration was, Welch wrote, "nervous." After the Indians had visited him, apprising him of the 1794 treaty, state officials quietly wrote their counterparts in Massachusetts and Washington, D.C., asking whether they knew anything about it. Nobody did. State officials thus became fearful that Reed might try to secure federal recognition for the tribe. The commissioner of the U.S. Bureau of Indian Affairs reassured state officials that there was nothing to substantiate a belief that any federal control over or financial responsibility for the Passamaquoddy Indians had ever existed. The surviving members of the tribe ultimately lost their ancestral lands.

In February 1970, a month after the 13-year-old stepdaughter of American Indian leader Richard Oakes fell to her death on Alcatraz Island, *Ramparts* published an essay titled "The Red Man's Burden," contributed by Peter Collier. Collier wrote about college students that had invaded Alcatraz Island in November 1969. The former prison had been abandoned, claiming ownership "by right of discovery," and citing an 1868 treaty allowing the Sioux possession of unused federal lands, American Indians decided to occupy the island. Under the Treaty of Fort Laramie between the U.S. and the Lakota, all retired, abandoned or out-of-use federal land was to be returned to the Native people who once occupied it.

Since Alcatraz penitentiary had been closed on March 21, 1963, and the island had been declared surplus federal property in 1964, a number of Red Power activists felt the island qualified for a reclamation. The Alcatraz Occupation made John Trudell, Richard Oakes, and LaNada Means symbols of the rights revolution and anti-colonialism inside the U.S. The occupation of the island was, however, forcefully ended by the federal government in June 1971. By the time Federal Marshall's arrived, only seven Indians were left on the island.

The Occupation of Alcatraz had a brief but somewhat direct effect on federal Indian Termination policies, and established a precedent for Indian activism and inspired later events, such as the occupation of the Bureau of Indian Affairs in Washington D.C. in

November 1972. Collier argued that the "Red Man's Burden" was white Americans trying to help them be more like white folks. "We need fewer and fewer 'experts' on Indians," Collier quoted author Vine Deloria. "What we need is a cultural leave-us-alone agreement, in spirit and in fact."[19]

Strangled in bureaucracy and swindled out of lands, forcibly alienated from his own culture, Collier wrote, the Indian continued in the early 1970s to be "victimized by the white man's symbolism." American Indians had

---

[19] Peter Collier, "The Red Man's Burden," *Ramparts Magazine*, February 1970, p. 30. Vine Victor Deloria Jr. was a Native American author, theologian, historian, and activist. He was widely known for his book Custer Died for Your Sins: An Indian Manifesto, which helped generate national attention to Native American issues in the same year as the Alcatraz-Red Power Movement. From 1964 to 1967, he had served as executive director of the National Congress of American Indians, increasing tribal membership from 19 to 156. Beginning in 1977, he was a board member of the National Museum of the American Indian, which now has buildings in both New York City and Washington, DC. He was influential in the development of what scientific critics called American Indian creationism, but which American Indians referred to as defenses against scientific racism.

been, Collier added, both "loved and hated to death." The Indian's "plight" had, Collier wrote, always inspired "recurrent orgies of remorse," but never had it forced white Americans to digest the implications of a nation and culture conceived in genocide. "We act as if the blood-debt of the past cannot be canceled until the Indian has no future," Collier concluded; "the guiltier he has made us, the more frantic have been the attempts to make him disappear."[20]

In the September 1970, *Ramparts* published a second story written by Collier titled "The Theft of a Nation: Apologies to the Cherokees." In it he depicted the Cherokee Nation of Oklahoma as having a colonial relationship with Phillips Oil. This was, Collier believed, due in large part to William Wayne "Bill" Keeler, the last appointed and first elected Principal Chief of the Cherokee Nation

---

[20] Ibid, p. 38.

in the 20th century. Educated as a chemical engineer, Keeler worked for Phillips Petroleum Company, where he became chief executive officer at the end of a long career with the company. He was one-sixteenth Cherokee, and throughout his life he also worked in the federal government for the advancement of Indians. President Harry Truman appointed him as Principal Chief of the Cherokee Nation of Oklahoma in 1949. Keeler also served as chairman for the executive committee of the Texas Cherokees and Associate Bands from 1939 until 1972.

In 1971, Keeler became the Cherokees' first elected chief since 1903. Some considered him to be the most influential person to the Cherokee nation aside from John Ross, who battled the removal of Indians and fought against the Cherokee Nation's forced relocation from Georgia to Oklahoma via the "Trail of Tears" in the nineteenth century. Keeler championed infrastructure building within Cherokee land as modernization and development concomitant to not promoting native sovereignty in the decades after World War II, which put him at odds with increasingly nationalistic Cherokee in the 1960s and 1970s. Keeler also argued that Indians should not be entitled to more rights than anybody else, but they should still have all the rights of everyone else.

His attitude jived nicely with the conservatism of white in Oklahomans, where Phillips, Keeler's former employer, owned a great deal of land, oil wells, and political power. In 1970, Collier wrote, the vast majority of Cherokee in that state lived "under the thumb of rural white Oklahoma and beneath the shadow of the Phillips 66 shield." Keeler, in short, seemed to Collier to be far more invested in defending the oil company than the

Cherokee, who Collier believed to have been colonized.[21]

In April 1971, *Ramparts* published yet another essay contributed by Collier titled "Salmon Fishing in America: The Indians vs. the State of Washington." Collier continued the theme of white Americans and their economic system devastating the remnants of what little of Native American cultural heritage and identity remained. Collier chronicled a group that called themselves the "Medicine Creek Nation," which was named in memory of the 1854 treaty that forfeited the rich Puget Sound area to the U.S. government.

The members of the group had begun to fish illegally along the Puyallup River in places where their ancestors had hundreds of years earlier. The Medicine Creek Nation was not fishing there, Collier explained, as a publicity

---

[21] Peter Collier, "The Theft of a Nation: Apologies to the Cherokees," *Ramparts Magazine*, September 1970, p. 45.

stunt or out of nostalgia for the past. They fished there because it was key to their survival. There were subsequent conflicts between Native Americans and authorities that, as Collier put it, "worked for the state of Washington" all through the 1960s, and which garnered national headlines that inspired "fish-ins" by the likes of actor Marlon Brando and comedian Dick Gregory. Despite the public attention, by 1971 matters had not improved for the Medicine Creek Nation. Their members were, Collier explained, of the Medicine routinely arrested. The increased vitriol and conflict between fish and wildlife authorities and the Native Americans fishing along the Puyallup River seemed, to Collier, to be a microcosm of the growing rift between leftists, liberals and conservatives in the early 1970s, a time in which violence and militancy was on the rise all across the nation.

After leaving Alcatraz early in 1970, Oakes became involved with the impoverished

Pit River Indians and their occupation of lands used by Pacific Gas and Electric, a northern California utility company, which they claimed were rightfully theirs. He also helped spur Native American studies in university curricula and was credited for helping to change U.S. federal government termination policies of Native American peoples and culture. In December 1972, two months after being shot and killed during an altercation with a YMCA director who Oakes believed to be abusive to Native American children, *Ramparts* published an essay written by him titled "Alcatraz is Not an Island." In it Oakes explained the reasons he and others had decided to occupy the island and laid out his vision of what his hopes and dreams were for a more egalitarian America.

His essay was followed immediately in the December 1972 edition of *Ramparts* by a eulogy contributed by Collier. In it Collier described the occupation of Alcatraz as "the moment when the Red Man finally stepped out from under the white bureaucrat's thumb and took control once again over his own life." He elaborated that Oakes "was not only a leader of this movement, but also probably the personification of the spirit of the island."[22] In many ways, Collier wrote, the passing of Alcatraz and Oakes marked an end to the era that had begun several years earlier with the fish-ins in Washington state, and had grown through the revolution of rising expectations fostered by programs of the Great Society. Indians had, Collier lamented, in some sense suddenly "ceased to be chic." But Oakes, Collier hailed, forced Americans to take a hard look at their own history and to better understand that it was founded on what Collier referred to as "a primal genocide against the Red Men." Indians had, he explained, "been rediscovered in a hot flash of

---

[22] Peter Collier, "The Only Good Indian..." *Ramparts Magazine*, December 1972, p. 36.

guilt before and always this same thing had happened: a shocked outcry, a few pieces of remedial legislation, some best-selling books, and then an echoing silence as the rhetoric about the 'plight' of the 'first Americans' ceased."[23] Collier concluded by expressing fear that as a symbol of revolution, Oakes' death might likely signal the beginning of the end of the Native Americans' rights revolution.

In January 1973, *Ramparts* published an essay titled "Bury My Heart on the Potomac: Indians at the BIA," contributed by Eugene L. Meyer, who was a reporter for *The Washington Post*. In early November 1972, just as President Richard Nixon had sealed a second-term (or so it seemed) in a landslide victory, American Indian Movement (AIM) leader Russell Means and eight-hundred and fifty American Indians

---

[23] Ibid, p. 37.

occupied the Bureau of Indian Affairs in Washington D.C.

The cadre had traveled in caravans along what they referred to as the "Trail of Broken Treaties." They had gathered peacefully to discuss grievances with the federal bureaucracy. But by the time they left the BIA, they had brought an institution of government to a complete standstill and, Meyer declared, left it a "shambles." A year and a half earlier, May Day protestors had come to Washington with precisely that purpose in mind and had been met with mass arrests and the suspension of police rules. The Indians, however, emerged from their confrontation "virtually unscathed, no busts and no heads busted," and were allowed to leave the building and the city under a signed "recommendation" for amnesty from the same

White House that had taken such a hard line on May Day 1971.24

AIM presented Nixon with their "Twenty Points," which established Native American goals for their relations with the federal government. Twelve of the twenty points directly or indirectly addressed treaty responsibility in which the U.S. had, AIM leaders believed, fallen short. The "Twenty Points" included:

1. Restoration of treaty making (ended by Congress in 1871).
2. Establishment of a treaty commission to make new treaties (with sovereign Native Nations).
3. Indian leaders to be permitted to address Congress.

---

24 Eugene L. Meyer, "Bury My Heart on the Potomac: Indians at the BIA," *Ramparts Magazine*, January 1973, p. 10.

4. Review of treaty commitments and violations.
5. Unratified treaties to go heard by the Senate for action.
6. All Indians to be governed by treaty relations.
7. Relief for Native Nations for treaty rights violations.
8. Recognition of the right of Indians to interpret treaties.
9. Joint Congressional Committee to be formed on reconstruction of Indian relations.
10. Restoration of 110 million acres of land taken away from Native Nations by the United States.
11. Restoration of terminated rights.
12. Repeal of state jurisdiction on Native Nations.
13. Federal protection for offenses against Indians.

14. Abolition of the Bureau of Indian Affairs.
15. Creation of a new office of Federal Indian Relations.
16. New office to remedy breakdown in the constitutionally prescribed relationships between the United States and Native Nations.
17. Native Nations to be immune to commerce regulation, taxes, trade restrictions of states.
18. Indian religious freedom and cultural integrity protected.
19. Establishment of national Indian voting with local options; free national Indian organizations from governmental controls
20. Reclaim and affirm health, housing, employment, economic development, and education for all Indian people.

When AIM left the Interior building of the BIA in November 1971, the White House had agreed to discuss all twenty points except amnesty, which was to be addressed separately. An "interagency task force" was later created, to be co-chaired by representatives of the White House and to include dozens of Indian organizations. The occupiers thus agreed to leave the BIA building with the assurance that the White House would examine eligibility of Indians for governmental services; adequacy of governmental service delivery; quality, speed, and effectiveness of federal programs; Indian self-government; and congressional implementation of necessary Indian legislation.

Nixon, Meyer explained, had a different opinion from the 1950s emphasis on termination of tribes and their governments. In line with ideas about decentralization of government, Nixon believed that tribes likely could do better than a distant government agency in managing affairs of their people and serving them. As such, in December 1973,

Nixon privately signed the Menominee Restoration Act, which returned Menominee Indians to full federally recognized tribal status, returning their land assets to trust status. Since this period, other terminated tribes regained their federally recognized status by Congressional legislation. In addition, other tribes achieved recognition, both through the BIA documentary process, which was a procedure developed in consultation with representatives of recognized tribes, and sometimes through direct Congressional action.

In June 1973, *Ramparts* published an interpretive report written by Collier titled "Wounded Knee: The New Indian War." In it he chronicled the events leading up to and surrounding what came to be known as the "Wounded Knee incident." It began on February 27, 1973, when approximately two hundred Oglala Lakota and followers of the American Indian Movement seized and occupied the town of Wounded Knee, South Dakota, on the Pine Ridge Reservation.

The protest followed the failure of an effort of the Oglala Sioux Civil Rights Organization to impeach tribal president Richard Wilson, whom they accused of corruption and abuse of power, including abuse of opponents. Additionally, protesters criticized the U.S. government's failure to fulfill treaties with Native American people and demanded the reopening of treaty negotiations. The FBI and U.S. Marshall's service were tasked with ending the uprising, which lasted from February until May 1973. Oglala and AIM activists controlled the town for seventy one days while federal agents and other law enforcement agencies cordoned off the area.

The activists chose the site of the 1890 Wounded Knee Massacre for its symbolic value. Both sides were armed, and shooting was frequent. A U.S. marshal was shot and paralyzed in March 1971. A Cherokee and an Oglala Lakota were also killed by shootings in April 1973. Ray Robinson, an African-American civil rights activist who joined the protesters, disappeared during the events and was believed to have been murdered. The occupation attracted wide media coverage, especially after the press accompanied both of South Dakota's U.S. senators from to Wounded Knee. The events galvanized many American Indians, who were inspired by the sight of Native Americans standing in defiance of the government which had so systemically abused them for centuries.

In March 1975, *Ramparts* published its last article explicitly addressing Native Americans' rights revolution. It was an essay titled "The Indian Movement: Out of a Wounded Past," contributed by Vine Deloria, a Standing Rock Sioux, who was born in Martin, South Dakota, a border town on the Pine Ridge

Reservation. Formerly Executive Director of the National Congress of American Indians, Deloria was the author of *Custer Died for Your Sins: An Indian Manifesto* (1969). The book was noteworthy for its relevance to the Alcatraz-Red Power Movement and other activist organizations, such as the American Indian Movement, which, in 1969, was beginning to expand.

Deloria's book encouraged better use of federal funds aimed at helping Native Americans. In "The Indian Movement: Out of a Wounded Past," Deloria noted the startling parallels between the violence waged against Native Americans in the nineteenth century and the war crimes in Vietnam, such as the My Lai Massacre. He argued that up until 1974 the Native Americans scored more legislative victories than any other movement in the rights revolution. From 1969 – 1974, Deloria noted, the Taos Pueblo had its Sacred Blue Lake restored to it. The claims of the Alaska

Natives, pending for more than a century, were finally resolved. Disputed lands taken by other government agencies in the early part of the century, such as those at Yakima and Warm Springs, had been returned. The Menominee tribe, which had been terminated from federal supervision, was restored to full federal services in 1973. The fishing rights struggle in the Pacific Northwest, which featured seemingly endless litigation and protest, resulted in a landmark decision in *United States v. Washington* (1973) in which the treaty fishing rights were upheld. Several very important income and sales tax cases were also won and Native Americans "held their own" in the very important field of water rights. Cases on affirmative action in employing Indians were also often decided favorably although, he conceded, the Bureau of Indian Affairs had been working hard to negate the effect. To be sure, the record of legal victories won by the Native American movement, both in litigation and legislation, was, Deloria asserted, very impressive, and when one considered the complexity of the field the success of Indians, he wrote, seemed "to be little short of miraculous."[25]

But there remained, he cautioned, an internal identity crisis amongst many Native Americans. "In many ways," he wrote, Indians participated in "the contemporary technical culture as much as other Americans." But very few Indians, he lamented, had come to realize how drastically this change affected the responsibility of their community as a whole to participate in the formation of a new American identity.[26] And despite their successes, Deloria added, and the buoyant optimism of many Indians about the future of the movement, prospects for the future seemed bleak.

---

[25] Vine Deloria Jr. "The Indian Movement: Out of a Wounded Past," *Ramparts Magazine*, March 1975, p. 30.

[26] Ibid, p. 31.

Looming on the horizon were, he explained, two world problems — famine and energy — which he feared would combine to crush the best efforts of Indians to continue moving forward. The guilt which white Americans had lavished on Indians in recent years was, he noted, rapidly being transferred to world famine. And the need for energy, when it really arrived, would demand that the government find a way to confiscate energy resources on Indian reservations.

"Guilt vanishes fast in a chilly office building in an energy-sparse urban society," he wrote. Both of these crises were, he predicted, moving to center stage of geopolitics much faster than affluent white folks seemed able to comprehend. And while Indians were at least aware of the energy crunch very few were, he regretted, able to comprehend how the "sight of starving millions on evening television would ultimately affect the attitude of American society towards its own poor and hungry."[27] He, however, expressed measured optimism that the Native Americans' rights revolution could be salvaged or whether it could cushion the shock which it would inevitably face if Indians could not understand their role in geopolitics.

But continued isolation on cultural grounds and withdrawing from participation in domestic movements, he warned, would simply result in making the vanishing American vanish once again. Instead of reconciling old differences, he wrote, and forgiving ideological heresies, or seeking out new allies on the domestic scene, many Indian leaders, he rued, seemed to want to remain aloof from current problems and continue to "recite the sins of the white man" and the non-Indian activities of the current crop of activists. But, he concluded, unless the movement forgave itself for being too successful and

---

[27] Ibid, p. 32.

concentrated on the consolidation of a new and better definition of America's responsibility to American Indians, the movement would likely degenerate into a fratricidal struggle for declining federal dollars and public attention — a tragic conclusion to a struggle that had come so far in such a short time.[28]

As successful as the Native Americans' rights revolution had been in the late-1960s and early 1970s, its trajectory mirrored that of so many other strains of the rights revolution, many of which lost momentum and cultural force in the wake of the end of the Vietnam War and the Watergate Scandal. The American retreat from Vietnam and Nixon's resignation signaled a retreat from the social activism which had played such a large role in shaping the history of that era. By the end of the Vietnam War and Watergate scandal, very many Americans, including very many who

---

[28] Ibid, p. 32.

had been activists or at least sympathetic to social movements, increasingly desired an end to the conflict and turmoil associated with the civil rights movement and Vietnam era in American history, opting instead for a retreat from the divisive identity politics that gradually fell by the wayside in the waning decades of the twentieth century. Many Americans, as evidenced by a conservative backlash that ushered in the rise of Ronald Reagan's America in the decades after Nixon's resignation and the end of the Vietnam War, sought a nostalgic return to the postwar "Affluent Society," which never actually existed for many Americans, namely millions of American Indians and African Americans who remained deprived of full citizenship in the waning decades of the twentieth century.

CHAPTER FOUR

"African Americans' Rights Revolution"

Ramparts Magazine was at the forefront of advocating civil rights for Americans, namely African Americans. For example, in December 1963, Ramparts, which was still a publication more committed to catering to a Roman Catholic Church readership than the counterculture, published four essays (three of which were written by white men) about the moral importance of the civil rights movement.

The first in the series was an essay penned by the Christian mystic Thomas Merton titled "The Black Revolution: Letters to a White Liberal." The rights revolution that African Americans were at the center of represented, Merton wrote, "a radical threat to our present system — a revolutionary situation."[29] He presciently foreshadowed what would become of the rights revolution if it were to become violent and militant when he explained how self-defeating militancy would

---

[29] Thomas Merton, "The Black Revolution," Ramparts Magazine, Christmas 1963, p. 11.

be to the civil rights movement in the midst of an increasingly militarized, violent, and overtly white supremacist society. It, Merton also predicted, was possible that as the civil rights movement gained in power, the reasonableness and the Christian fervor of these elements might "recede into the background and the movement would become more and more an unreasoning and intransigent mass movement dedicated to the conquest of sheer power, more and more inclined to violence."[30] Merton thus called for a complete reform of the American social system, which, he asserted, permitted and bred such deep-seated racial injustices. This work of reorganization, he explained, had to be carried out under "the inspiration of the Negro whose providential time" had finally arrived, and who had "received from God enough light,

---

[30] Ibid, p. 17.

ardor and spiritual strength to free the white man in freeing himself from the white man."[31]

Merton's "Letter to White Liberals" was followed in the December 1963 edition of *Ramparts* by an essay contributed by John Howard Griffen titled "Journal of a Trip South." In it Griffen chronicled a Roman Catholic priest who had spent a week meeting and greeting both black and white folks in the Deep South, a region in which white supremacy was perhaps more conspicuous than other parts of the nation. Griffen noted that he had often broke Jim Crow propriety by meeting with black folks in their homes during his trip. As such, he discovered firsthand how deeply racist law enforcement was, noting how the police often followed him from town to town in order to menace him.

"Journal of a Trip South" was followed by an essay titled "Faulkner on Race,"

---

[31] Ibid, p. 20.

contributed by Bradford Daniel, who was a Texas-based journalist and a former white editor of *Sepia Magazine*.[32] Faulkner, the Nobel Prize-winning author, Bradford wrote, dedicated his literary career to analyzing and evaluating universal problems in the provincial setting of Northern Mississippi. Ignoring moonlight and magnolia, Faulkner instead pictured the South as a way of life that had disappeared forever, a region haunted by memories of the past and fearful of a commercialized future that Faulkner believed would make life impersonal and depthless. "He loved the South as much as any man," Bradford wrote, "yet he was never afflicted with the Southern malady of being blinded by its prejudices and faults."[33] Faulkner was not,

---

[32] *Sepia* was a photojournalistic magazine styled like *Look* and sometimes compared to *Ebony*. It featured articles based primarily on achievements of African Americans. It was part of the rise of postwar publications and businesses aimed at black audiences.

[33] Bradford Daniel, "Faulkner on Race," *Ramparts Magazine*, Christmas 1963, p. 43.

Bradford added, a "South Hater" nor a white supremacist. Faulkner, Bradford concluded, seemed hopeful that the literary genius he described in his essay might serve as a paragon to the rest of the region's white inhabitants.

The final essay published in the December 1963 edition of *Ramparts* was titled "The Marginal Man." It was written by Thomas N. Williams, a man who described himself as a half-black and half-white Chicago native. Williams was also a graduate of Stanford University, an administrative assistant to a California school district, and an officer of the local Catholic Interracial Council. His essay elaborated the identity crisis of being mixed-race in America.

"Despite the presence of quarts of white blood," he wrote, "in this country I am a Negro and I always will be, equally by the grace of God and by the insistence of the great white segment of American society." The fact is, he added, "I am a marginal man, not entirely

Negro and yet not white."34 The two worlds of black and white that existed in American society, he explained, were separated. To be on the fringe of both of those worlds, not fully incorporated into either, and still to be a basic part of both, was, he explained, his destiny. But facing one's fears meant, he noted, evaluating one's self in terms of one's beliefs and the purposes of one's life. "This is," he wrote, "what I as a marginal man have had to do to survive. This is what all of us must do if our society is to survive. This is what the Negro revolution is forcing the white world to do at this moment in history." This was why, he explained, African Americans could potentially be the "salvation of the white man in the United States," and "save him from the fate of drowning in his own apathy."35

---

34 Thomas N. Williams, "The Marginal Man," *Ramparts Magazine*, Christmas 1963, p. 50.

35 Ibid, p. 56.

Bradford contended that that every American should become marginal men, marginal in the spiritual sense, by subverting their prejudices to their religious beliefs. "The challenge to become marginal" was, he explained, "there for all of us" in the sense that Americans most desperately needed to open themselves more in order to let in the "meaning and force of the Christian faith that would project them into that no-man's-land" where there was "scant refuge and great suspicion," and, he concluded, "where love for one another may well cost us some friends, but will gain for us eternal salvation."[36]

In October 1964, *Ramparts* published a special report written by executive editor Warren Hinckle titled "The March That Failed." In July of 1964, Harlem in New York was rocked by riots after James Powell was shot and killed by police Lieutenant Thomas

---

[36] Ibid, p. 56.

Gilligan. The second bullet of three fired by Gilligan killed Powell, who was a 15-year-old African American boy sitting on a stoop with his friends. Immediately after the shooting, about three hundred students from a nearby school who were informed by the principal spontaneously rallied in a show of support for the slain teenager and as a protest against the officer who killed him.

The shooting set off six consecutive nights of rioting that affected the New York City neighborhoods of Harlem and Bedford-Stuyvesant. In total, four thousand New Yorkers participated in the riots, some of which included vandalism, looting, and attacks on New York City Police officers. At the end of the conflict, reports counted one dead rioter, one-hundred and eighteen injured, and four-hundred and sixty five arrests.

Later that summer, Hinckle explained, The Progressive Labor Movement, which was led by William Epton, planned to march along Lennox Avenue to protest endemic white supremacy in the NYPD. The PLM had what Hinkle described as "a rag-bag ideology of Chinese-style Communism, African nationalism, black supremacy, and Marxist-Leninist theorizing." Its goals were "vague," but its tactics were "uncompromisingly tough."[37]

This toughness was apparent on the Saturday following the days of bloody rioting in Harlem, when the PLM announced plans for a new mass demonstration which police were sure would spark more rioting. The "black establishment" — as the black radicals called them, the major Negro groups, CORE, NAACP, other established civil rights organizations, Negro churchmen and Harlem businessmen, met to squelch the march

---

[37] Warren Hinckle, "The March That Failed," *Ramparts Magazine*, October 1964, p. 30.

because they feared it would bring new violence to the streets and further weaken what Hinckle referred to as the Black Establishment's "faltering hold on the unhappy people of Harlem."[38] Their plan, which foreshadowed tactics used by the FBI in the COINTELPRO program, was to permit one of the splinter black nationalist groups in Harlem to break up the march by starting a fight, which would force the white police force to jail members of the PLM. Many members of the PLM wanted to march and fight anyway. Epton, however, explained that being goaded into violence against other black folks was exactly what the white power structure and the "Black Establishment" members in their pockets wanted.

In November 1964, Hinckle contributed another report titled "The Sorrowful Mysteries of the Negro Catholic." In it Hinckle chronicled

---

[38] Ibid.

a barber in Los Angeles, California. The barber was named Leon Aubrey. He was in a struggle with his Cardinal, James Francis McIntyre of Los Angeles. Aubrey was, Hinckle explained, the leader of a group of Negro Catholics who had taken their grievances against the Cardinal's peculiar stance on race relations to the streets. The group had paraded in front of the foreboding portals of exclusive Fremont Place, the site of the Cardinal's residence, and picketed the Los Angeles Chancery Office. The racist Cardinal tried to get Aubrey's business shut down, which, Hinckle believed, underscored the inveterate white supremacy in the Roman Catholic Church in Southern California in the 1960s. McIntrye's efforts to close the barbershop also, Hinckle believed, underscored the endemic abuse of power that was common to McIntyre's cardinalship. Hinckle's essay also demonstrated his spiritual drift from Catholicism in reaction to the Church's overt hypocrisy. It also signaled the magazine's gradual drift from the Church toward the budding counterculture.

The theme of the Roman Catholic Church's racist hypocrisy was a theme in the December 1964 edition of *Ramparts,* most notably in an essay titled "Magnolia Ghetto: Report from New Orleans," written by John Beecher, who was a poet that taught at the University of Santa Clara in California. Beecher illuminated that white supremacy was entrenched in the Catholic Church, especially in the Deep South. In 1890, he noted, about eighty percent of New Orleans' African Americans were Catholic. The first segregated church was established against African Americans' bitter opposition in 1895.

By 1965, Beecher added, just twenty-five percent of the New Orleans black population was Catholic. This was, he wrote, a consequence of the Church going along with the segregationist tide of the 1890's. He also noted that there was not one black priest in any of New Orleans' thirteen parishes. The Church's schools were also racially segregated and by no means equal. Holy Ghost, for example, a black school, had just fifteen teachers for a student body of seven-hundred and forty six, a ratio of one to fifty compared to St. James Major, a white school that had twenty six teachers for seven-hundred and eighty three students, a ratio of one to thirty.

The qualifications and credentials of teachers in the black schools were also, Beecher explained, often inferior to those in the white schools of the archdiocese. Physical facilities of the black Catholic schools were also, he added, "usually deplorably second-rate." As such, Beecher concluded, "Despite all the talk in the Catholic Church about reform in the early 1960s, the hierarchy of the organization seemed keen to "talk of the human family and Christ's love as they did the Devil's work of maintaining and profiting from a system of social inequality," which was a "scaffolding the Church had helped to build during slavery and the Jim Crow era."[39]

In April 1965, *Ramparts* published a pictorial essay with text written by Beecher with photos contributed by Michael Alexander titled "Black Mammies of Royal Street." It was about obscene effigies of black mammies, a hateful stereotype, that darkened the doorways of shops along Royal Street in the Vieux Carre section of New Orleans. Ironically, Beecher explained, the police would pick up any African American with no business to be on Royal Street but the pejorative and racist effigies comparable to wooden Indian Chiefs outside a tobacco shop were considered charming and designed to lure tourists into shops.

In June 1965, *Ramparts* dedicated almost the entire issue to making sense of the March 7, 1965 March on Selma, Alabama, which was

---

[39] John Beecher, "Magnolia Ghetto: Report from New Orleans," *Ramparts Magazine*, December 1964, p. 43.

marred by white supremacist police brutality of protestors. The first piece in the series was an editorial that linked anti-colonialism in Vietnam to the civil rights revolution in the U.S. titled "Our 'Niggers' in Asia." The essay set the stage for a series of articles published in the same edition titled "The South at War" that chronicled the violence of the civil rights march from Selma to Montgomery, Alabama.

In Selma, voting rolls were ninety-nine percent white and one percent African American, while the 1960 Census found that the population of Alabama was thirty percent nonwhite. In February 1965, state troopers and locals in Marion, Alabama, started an armed confrontation with some four hundred unarmed African American demonstrators. Jimmie Lee Jackson, a black man, was shot in the stomach. He died eight days later. As word spread about the atrocity, the case alarmed civil rights activists, including Martin Luther King Jr. and James Bevel, both of whom were members of the Southern Christian Leadership Conference.

Bevel, SCLC's Director of Direct Action, strategized a plan for a peaceful march on the state's capitol, which required crossing the Edmund Pettus Bridge. On March 7, 1965, armed police attacked peaceful civil rights demonstrators attempting to march to Montgomery in an incident that became known as Bloody Sunday. Because of the design of the bridge, the protesters were unable to see the police officers on the east side of the bridge until after they had reached the top of it, which was one hundred feet above the Alabama River. Despite the potential for danger ahead, the protesters continued to march. They were then attacked and beaten by police on the other side.

Televised images of the brutal attack presented Americans and international audiences with horrifying images of marchers left bloodied and severely injured as tear gas wafted through the air. In all, seventeen marchers were hospitalized. The marches were organized by nonviolent activists to demonstrate the desire of African-American citizens to exercise their constitutional right to vote, in defiance of segregationist repression, and were part of a broader voting rights movement underway in Selma and throughout the American South.

By highlighting racial injustice, the intrepid marchers contributed to passage that year of the Voting Rights Act, a landmark federal achievement of the civil rights movement. Selma and all that had followed, the editors of *Ramparts* explained, revealed a most tragic inconsistency in the American concept of justice. Now that African Americans had fought and won federal protection for their basic human right to vote for the politicians that supposedly represented them, it further underscored that the U.S. had,

Ramparts editors noted, actively prevented the Vietnamese from holding elections due to the fact that Ho Chi Minh would have surely been elected to represent the Vietnamese People.

As of June 1965, the editors noted, no elections had been held in Vietnam and no election would be held as long as there was any possibility that such an election might prove an embarrassment to American neo-colonialist ambitions. The editors explained that preventing democracy in both Vietnam and the American South underscored the hypocrisy of America waging war in Vietnam for any reason but to serve the economic and political interests of American politicians and the corporations they represented; but thwarting democracy also undermined the U.S. because, as the editors wrote, "No nation can stand the test of time if that nation is not founded on justice, as distinct from pseudo-justice that grants to one what it withholds from another." Selma and South Vietnam was, the editors added, "there for all the world to see."40 The editors concluded optimistically that now that the U.S. had seemingly committed itself to honoring the humanity of African Americans by passing the Voting Rights Act, that perhaps the Vietnamese would soon also be perceived as human beings entitled to the same rights as everyone else.

That editorial was followed by the first part of "The South at War" series. The first essay in it was titled "The Yellow Rose of Texas," which was contributed by Edward M. Keating. It was, Keating noted, no mere coincidence that virtually the last battle of the Civil War took place in Selma, Alabama, since the latest battle of Selma was, he asserted, an example that The South was "still in secession" and the Civil War had not yet ended.41 The

---

40 *Ramparts* editorial staff, "Our 'Niggers' in Asia," *Ramparts Magazine*, June 1965, p. 4.

41 Edward M. Keating, "Introduction: The Yellow Rose of Texas," *Ramparts Magazine*, June 1965, p. 17.

South, he further noted, "once cried for secession; now it cries for 'States Rights;'" in both instances the desired end had been power to keep black folks in a state of servitude. "States' Rights" was, Keating believed, the South's "indispensable bargaining tool in negotiating national policy with the rest of the country, which ostensibly kept southern blacks firmly in their place paying taxes into a political system that ensured their second-class citizenship. State's Rights was, Keating believed, racially coded opposition to Earl Warren's Supreme Court and also to the federal government passing the Civil Rights and Voting Rights Act. The rhetoric of States' Rights also helped to explain the region's overwhelming support of Arizona Senator Barry Goldwater in the 1964 general election and the success of Richard Nixon's Southern Strategy in 1968.

Keating's essay was followed by a series of maps titled "Five Battles of Selma." In it he underscored continuity between the American Civil War with the civil rights movement of the 1960s. The maps, for example, showed where violence was waged in and around Selma during both conflicts.

The maps linking the Civil War and civil rights movement was followed by five essays written by editors Warren Hinckle and David Welsh titled "Battle of the Bridge," "Show of Force," "Charge of the Bible Brigade," "The Infiltration," and the "Shadow Brigade," all of which provided an incredibly in depth blow-by-blow account of the police assault on nonviolent protesters near the Edmund Pettus Bridge, and also illuminated the historical and social significance of the events of February and March 1965 in both a national and global context.

The editors, however, lamented that the Voting Rights Bill did no more than promise African Americans what they had already won a century earlier (which history proved was as much a setback for the race as evidence of progress). The essayists thus urged readers to temper their optimism with cautious vigilance. They further argued that President Johnson hoped that his new bill would "get the Negroes" off the streets. Hinckle and Welch, however, presciently concluded that "next the Negroes will go into the streets over jobs, housing, getting the schools really integrated." That was, they concluded, the real "strategic lesson of the Battle of Selma."[42] In other words, the Civil Rights and Voting Rights Acts were but small battles won, but the revolution had only just begun.

In September 1965, *Ramparts* published an editorial titled "SNCC Marching Orders" that underscored how dangerous things seemed for leaders of the Student Non-Violent Coordinating Committee civil rights workers

---

[42] Warren Hinckle and David Welsh, "The South at War: The Shadow Brigade," *Ramparts Magazine*, June 1965, p. 52.

in Jackson, Mississippi. The editorial elaborated that security regulations set forth in SNCC's Security Bulletin, which was issued to all Jackson workers, cautioned that traveling at night should be avoided; that members should also avoid sleeping near windows; and there was strict orders to not drink alcohol. Failing to adhere to the guidelines, the bulletin warned, could put members' lives and the credibility of SNNC's projects and efforts in grave danger.

In October 1965, *Ramparts* published an essay titled "Free-Lance Integrationist" about a Chicago, Illinois public school teacher named John J. Walsh, written by Lewis Z. Koch, who was a producer at *CBS-TV* in Chicago. In 1964 Walsh purchased a home in Mayor Richard Daley's racially segregated suburban Chicago neighborhood of Bridgeport. In an attempt to integrate the neighborhood, Walsh attracted black Chicagoans to live on his property.

Walsh's effort attracted a great deal of protest amongst Bridgeport's white residents who felt as though they were, as Walsh put it, being invaded. A number of mob actions and arrests into 1965, he explained, created a situation in which the African American postal clerk who lived in Walsh's house on Lowe Street felt imperiled, and eventually moved. Walsh's attempt to integrate Daley's neighborhood ultimately failed to do anything but stoke the ire of white property owners and terrify black residents. White terrorism had, in short, been an effective means and method of maintaining the racial status quo in Mayor Daley's neighborhood.

In November 1965, *Ramparts* published an essay titled "Massah LBJ and His Nigrahs," written by Saul Landau. He argued that although African Americans had won the right to vote, they were still denied full economic and social equality all across the nation. African Americans remained, in short, largely second-class citizens. The ability to vote, Landau explained, did not provide a member of the polity with meaningful choices; at best, he wrote, it was "the lesser of two evils."[43] He argued that President Johnson's Voting Rights Act did quite little to genuinely alter the racial power structure and dynamic that had long existed in the U.S. In fact, Landau argued, black folks winning the right to vote was actually a ploy to consolidate the African-American vote so that Johnson could continue to wage war in Vietnam. In short, though African Americans had won the right to vote, it was but a means of maintaining white supremacy at home and abroad.

In November 1965, *Ramparts* published an essay titled "The Liberator," contributed by Truman Nelson, who was the author of three historical novels. His profile published in *Ramparts* chronicled the nineteenth century abolitionist activism of William Lloyd

---

[43] Saul Landau, "Massah LBJ and His Nigrahs," *Ramparts Magazine*, November 1965, p. 10.

Garrison, who was perhaps best known as one of the founders of the American Anti-Slavery Society and as editor of *The Liberator,* an abolitionist newspaper.

Garrison, Nelson explained, promoted "immediate emancipation" of all slaves in the U.S., as opposed to the gradual emancipation championed by moderates. Nelson's profile of Garrison and his muckraking newspaper continued the theme that the American Civil War had never really ended and that the Civil Rights Revolution was by no means over; it was, rather, an ever evolving and shape shifting conflict.

The beauty and the triumph of William Lloyd Garrison, Nelson wrote, was that he tried to develop the goodness, the tenderness, of man and have it overcome the badness. Garrison could not, Nelson explained, stay in a sect or a church in which people vowed every Sunday to uphold the rule of Christ on earth and then hate and degrade their brothers every other day of the week. Garrison could not, Nelson added, give loyalty to a country which promised freedom and equality as an absolute and yet dealt out slavery and exceptionalism, and worshipped property as a god.[44] The reader also was provided the sense that Nelson believed *Ramparts* was carrying on *The Liberator's* legacy of high-minded muckraking.

In July 1966, *Ramparts* published an essay titled "A Government of the Black," contributed by Christopher Jencks and Milton Kotler, both of whom were resident fellows at the Institute for Policy Studies in Washington, D.C. There had, they lamented, been a marked decrease in the visible and news-making forms of protest: sit-ins, protest marches and picket lines. Then, just as the movement seemed to be gaining victories in the form of national legislation like the 1965 Voting Rights Act,

---

[44] Truman Nelson, "The Liberator," *Ramparts Magazine*, November 1965, p. 29.

there appeared, Jencks and Kottler feared, increasing signs of political disunity in the movement.

In Lowndes County, Alabama, they explained, the Student Non-violent Coordinating Committee, which was led by Stokely Carmichael, organized an all-black political party, which stoked criticism from the more moderate SCLC, including Martin Luther King Jr. At its 1965 convention, SNCC also reshuffled its leadership and moved in the direction of more militancy and greater emphasis on a black orientation within the organization.

These events, Jencks and Kotler believed, signified more than a mere factional struggle in the civil rights movement. They were symptoms of an underlying conflict over political strategy that they presciently believed would undermine the movement. Jencks and Kotler, however, understood the logic of African Americans taking more direct action in terms of black leadership to lead the movement. Racism had, they noted, corrupted Southern government to a point where it could not possibly incorporate people into equality. As such, political equality in the South, they asserted, required a new beginning, a reconstruction and renewal of American political institutions that amounted to reconstitution. "Negroes," Jencks and Kotler believed, needed to "take the lead in such a renewal." The essayists, in short, believed that America needed to begin the arduous task of renewing all of its institutions, in order to bring people together in political equality, and rediscover a form of government that could truly represent and serve everyone.

In November 1966, *Ramparts* published a series of essays titled "White Power." The first essay in the series was titled "White Power Illustrated." It was contributed by creative director Dugald Stermer. The essay included collage-like images of white folks in positions of prominence and power, including astronauts, George Washington, Mother Mary, the Pope, and law enforcement officers.

"White Power Illustrated" was followed in the November 1966 edition of *Ramparts* by an essay written by Gene Marine titled "I've Got Nothing Against the Colored." Marine traveled around Chicago interviewing white Catholics in the city about the conservative backlash that was manifesting itself in the form of white residents jeering, and throwing rocks and bottles, and some waving Nazi flags or wearing Ku Klux Klan robes to protest marches led by African Americans.

"I wish they were all Nazis," Marine confessed. That way one could "understand that sickness and attempt to cure it."[45] The white Chicagoans he interviewed couched their white supremacy in a language of "reverse racism" and protection of property

---

[45] Gene Marine, "I've Got Nothing Against the Colored," *Ramparts Magazine*, November 1966, p. 13.

rights to defend their inveterate privilege and sense of white supremacy. "The surest way to get belted in the mouth right now" was, Marine concluded, "to walk up to me and say you've got nothing against the colored."[46]

His essay underscored that the civil rights movement seemed to in many ways make white supremacy more intractable by making it more subtle and concealed. In other words, the civil rights movement further entrenched white supremacy by couching racism in racially coded language in which indigent African Americans were increasingly depicted as villainous welfare chiselers and inclined toward criminality in contrast to white supremacists who cast themselves as victims of a communistic War on Poverty and Great Society that they perceived to be as "reverse racism." An interesting aspect of Marine's essay is his chronicling of European migrants from places like Lithuania and Bohemia

---

[46] Ibid, p. 18.

increasingly deciding to vote Republican based on the notion that East Coast liberals and poor blacks were in a kind of Faustian alliance against working class white folks in cities such as Chicago, which foreshadowed the rise of Richard Nixon's Southern Strategy.

In May 1968, *Ramparts* published a series of reports titled "In White America." The first in the series was an editorial titled "The Execution of Dr. King" that echoed Stokely Carmichael's ominous warning that white America had sealed its own fate by murdering the apostle of non-violence. The editorial prophesied very dark days ahead in terms of race relations in the U.S. The reader was provided a great sense of the anger and despair of the editors, whose wounds were still very fresh and whose anger and despair were at a peak.

The essay "The Execution of Dr. King" was followed by an editorial penned by Eldridge Cleaver titled "Requiem for

Nonviolence." In it he openly advocated armed revolution as the only logical next step in the civil rights revolution. "Requiem for Nonviolence" was followed by an editorial contributed by Gene Marine titled "Getting Eldridge Cleaver" in which he tried to elaborate Cleaver's rage and advocating of violence to well-intentioned non-violent white liberals.

"Getting Eldridge Cleaver" was followed by another essay written by Cleaver titled "The Land Question." In it he argued that there would never be any true justice or equality in the U.S. until black men and women could own their own land and carve out an existence free of the capitalist system which had systemically entrenched African Americans into second-class citizenship. In other words, he demanded the forty acres and a mule that had been promised to black folks at the conclusion of the Civil War, which, Marine argued, had never actually ended.

In December 1968, *Ramparts* published a review of David Weiss's documentary, *No Vietnamese Ever Called Me Nigger* (1968), which had won first prize at the Mannheim Film Festival in Germany. The review was contributed by Art Goldberg, who had seen the film at the San Francisco Film Festival.

The movie was filmed at a 1967 anti-war march in New York City, specifically from Harlem to the United Nations on the occasion of Martin Luther King Jr.'s speech at the United Nations. King famously questioned the disproportionate percentage of black compared to white soldiers in combat in Vietnam. On-street interviews with black residents of Harlem were interlaced with the comments of three black soldiers who had recently returned from the war. Few of those interviewed, Goldberg wrote, were disturbed by Bayard Rustin's charges that King was unwise to try to unite the civil rights and antiwar movements, for many of the interviewees had already seen that black soldiers were bearing the brunt of the casualties "fighting for freedom" in Vietnam and then coming back to an America that was "far from free."[47]

At a time when more moderate civil rights activists such as Roy Wilkins and Whitney Young were condemning Reverend King for speaking out against the war, Weiss' film showed that many of the people sitting on Harlem's tenement steps and lounging in ghetto doorways were keenly aware that the government was dumping billions of dollars into destroying Vietnam while the black communities in the U.S. were rapidly decaying and growing more violent. One of the interviewees in the film was a young Marine Corps veteran named Achmed Lorence. He particularly seemed to draw a connection between the plight of the Vietnamese and

---

[47] Art Goldberg, "Document the Ghetto: A review of David Weiss' documentary, *No Vietnamese Ever Called Me Nigger*," *Ramparts Magazine*, December 14, 1968, p. 63.

African Americans. He also realized that the white Marines would be returning to a vastly different America than he would. "Do you really think they're going to put some of that money they've been wasting in Viet-Nam into our communities when the war is over?" Lorence asked Weiss. "Are you kidding? They'd rather spend it on sending a man to the moon."[48]

In October 1969, *Ramparts* published a book review titled "Publishing the Black Experience," contributed by Michael Thelwell, who was teaching black literature at Cornell at the time of publication. He reviewed three recently published books that delved into African-American culture: William Styron's *Nat Turner: Ten Black Writers Respond* (1968); Edward Margolies, *Native Sons: A Critical Study of Twentieth Century Negro American Authors* (1968); and James A. Emanuel and Theodore

---

[48] Ibid, p. 64.

Gross' *Dark Symphony: Negro Literature in America* (1968). Thelwell's review continued the theme of giving voice to African Americans, arguably the most marginalized group of people in American history.

In *Nat Turner: Ten Black Writers Respond*, the authors collectively argued that Styron, a white author, had suppressed some facts about the real Nat Turner while inventing others. The ten essays were contributed by various members of the black intelligentsia (among them John O. Kittens and John H. Williams), and one piece that discussed the almost wholly admiring review coverage of the book in the mainstream (white) American press. Styron's book was, the ten essayists agreed to various degrees, mired in misinterpretation. They, like Thelwell, seemed especially bothered by Nat Turner being depicted as a white supremacist's stereotyped sexual threat to white womanhood.

Native Sons: A Critical Study of Twentieth Century Negro American Authors provided a very useful analysis of twentieth-century African-American literature and contained chapters that examined sixteen authors: W.E.B. DuBois, Charles W. Chesnutt, James W. Johnson, Paul L. Dunbar, Langston Hughes, Jean Toomer, Claude McKay, and Countee Cullen, William Attaway, Richard Wright, Chester Himes, James Baldwin Ralph Ellison, and Malcolm X.

Dark Symphony: Negro Literature in America was similar to *Native Sons*, but cast a wider historical net, focusing on nineteenth century luminaries such as Frederick Douglass, the runaway slave turned renowned abolitionist. These texts collectively helped to illuminate the flowering of African-American studies in 1960s liberal arts and humanities academies. The scarcity of black female authors in *Native Sons* and *Dark Symphony*, however, underscored the fact that black women's voiced in American history, such as the voice of Sojourner Truth and Ida B. Welles, were still very much muted, even amongst otherwise progressive scholars such as Thelwell.

In July 1971, *Ramparts* published an essay titled "Battle for the South: Phase Two," Contributed by Charles Fulwood, who had worked with the Revolutionary Nationalist movement in the South and on the East Coast since 1967. In "Battle for the South" Fulwood argued that the rise in black nationalist sentiment in the South was the result of years of racial segregation.

Forced integration in the early 1970s, he explained, increasingly forced black students into predominately white environments where they were viewed as "intruding minorities" and thus suffered the full intensity of racist hatred. One "tragic result" of the closing of black schools and busing blacks kids to suburban schools to achieve what he referred to as racial balance was that scores of black administrators and instructors had been left jobless in the wake of the Nixon civil rights "progress," because the integrated school systems tended to regard them as having been educated at "inferior" institutions, and therefore not properly qualified to teach in racially integrated situations. "The endless pieties about 'separate but equal' which were used to defend the old segregated system," Fulwood wrote, "were thus exposed for all their hypocritical emptiness" in Florida.[49]

Fulwood provided two case studies: the desegregation of schools in Gainesville and St. Petersburg, Florida, to illustrate the nature of the struggle to defend black institutions that had developed. In both cities, Africans Americans fought hard to keep their schools open, arguing that the integration movement had been totally misconstrued as an effort to associate black folks with supposedly

---

[49] Charles Fulwood, "Battle For The South: Phase Two," *Ramparts Magazine*, July 1971, p. 37.

culturally superior white folks, rather than to achieve true equality. With the support of the black community, ninety percent of the student body at Gainesville's former black high school staged a walk-out and launched an organizing campaign in the hopes of inspiring more consistent marches and sundry other public protests.

Many parents also accompanied their children to school board meetings, demanding the maintenance of the academic standard of the school. After two weeks of tension and unrest, a federal court approved the Alachua County school board's decision and Nixon's "racial balance" program was implemented in Gainesville. As had been predicted, hostility sharpened between white instructors and black students, and among the students themselves. Racial tension, Fulwood noted, had been growing at a steady pace in Gainesville when the "inevitable explosion occurred."[50] As a

---

[50] Ibid.

gesture of contempt for the black students, a group of white pupils calling themselves the "KKK" raised the confederate flag on the school's flagpole. When black students attempted to stop the white students from hoisting the stars and bars, a small-scale "riot" erupted.

In addition to the stewing racial conflict in Gainesville, Fulwood also examined the rise of the Junta of Militant Organizations (JOMO), which was founded in St. Petersburg, Florida in 1968 in the wake of the assassination of Martin Luther King Jr. JOMO claimed to have no ambitions of becoming a vanguard organization, but rather sought to build a grassroots movement. The rise of JOMO and the backlash to integration in Gainesville and Saint Petersburg indicated, to Fulwood, the new mood of black militancy that was inflamed by Nixon's "racial balance" campaign in Deep South states such as Florida.

In November 1974, *Ramparts* published another essay written by Charles Fulwood titled "Blacks for Wallace." In it he chronicled the support given by African Americans to Governor George Wallace of Alabama, a man who in 1963 infamously declared "segregation now, segregation tomorrow, segregation forever." Wallace had, however, slightly softened his stance since being shot and paralyzed below the waste in 1972 and as a result of the state's black majority being more enfranchised in the early 1970s.

In the wake of the assassination attempt, Wallace tried to forge new alliances with black leaders. And although it appeared on the surface that Wallace was ready to play fair game with black voters it was, Fulwood warned, ludicrous to assume that he would repudiate his fundamental stand on social and political issues at the risk of losing his more important white conservative and racist base. Fulwood expressed deep regret that a "crackpot realism" had seemingly gained center stage for some of the South's leading black politicians. Fulwood reminded readers that as recently as 1965 Wallace was the man who ordered Alabama State Troopers and Sheriff Jim Clark into the streets of Birmingham to violently quell civil rights protests. Nothing thus, in Fulwood's mind, justified African Americans' political support of Wallace. The essay also illuminated the tragedy and farce of black accommodation to white supremacists.

That theme continued in the December 1974 edition of *Ramparts*. The editors published a series of nine essays about desegregation busing, which was the practice of assigning and transporting students to schools in such a manner as to redress prior racial segregation of schools, or to overcome the effects of residential segregation on local school demographics. The first essay in the "Busing" series was titled "Busing into Southie," written by Andrew Kopkind. In 1965, Kopkind explained, Massachusetts passed into law the Racial Imbalance Act, which ordered school districts to desegregate or risk losing state educational funding. The first law of its kind in the nation, it was opposed by many in Boston, especially less-well-off white ethnic areas, such as the Irish-American neighborhood of South Boston, where violence erupted. The troubles in Southie, Kopkind noted, grew from ancient grudges and a bitterness beyond the battles of the day.

Before busing, before desegregation, before black emigration from Dixie, South Boston was a racial and class ghetto where the Yankee brahmins contained the unruly Irishmen who intruded on the old genteel order. Like the dwellers of all ghettoes, the men and women of Southie were, Kopkind asserted, burdened with a combative pride that struck wildly at every real slight or imagined threat from outside. Threatened and fearful, the people of Southie would, Kopkind wrote, attack anyone who "diminished the integrity of their poor world and meager lives."[51] In Boston, busing fanned the flames a vitriolic racism that had been dormant under the high moral tone of America's civil rights years, but it re-emerged in its most explicit and aggressive forms in reaction to forced integration. Busing had thus become a codeword for a multitude of goals and sins. Deep divisions over race, class, communities, private aspirations, and social mobility were involved, Kopkind concluded, and converged on the battlefield of public education.

Kopkind's essay was followed by an eight-part symposium about busing. The first was written by Herb Kohl, who was the author of *Half the House* (1974). Kohl argued that the residents of Southie were correct in cherishing

---

[51] Andrew Kopkind, "Busing into Southie," *Ramparts Magazine*, December 1974, p. 38.

their culture, but pride in one's own culture did not, he asserted, require that group to oppress others.

Kohl's article was followed by John Holt's entry in the symposium. Holt was a writer and lecturer and the author of six books including *Escape from Childhood* (1974), which focused on his beliefs about the rights of children in society in general rather than schooling specifically. The book advocated for youth rights and against what Holt referred to as "adultism." He, like Kopkind and Kohl, believed the white backlash stoked by busing from California to Maine was evidence of status anxiety amongst low-income white folks who feared being further marginalized as a result of Nixon's "racial balance" plan. Poor people did not, Holt lamented, worry much about the need for racial understanding. "Most of all," he concluded, they worried that nobody on Capitol Hill or in the canyons of Wall Street really cared about their concerns or best interest of their kids.52 In other words, poor white Americans channeled their resentment towards the white folks who oppressed them into violence (both real and symbolic) against non-white minorities.

Holt's contribution to the symposium was followed in the December 1974 edition of *Ramparts* by Noel Day's essay. Day helped to organize the school boycotts in Boston in the mid-1960s and was a co-founder of the Boston Freedom Schools in 1963-64. He seconded Kohl's status anxiety thesis. "Instead of pushing for a bigger share of society's wealth," Day lamented, white people in cities like Boston were "fighting over the leavings," which Day perceived to be the real "tragedy of Boston" — the fact that white Bostonians

---

52 John Holt, "Busing: A Symposium," *Ramparts Magazine*, December 1974, p. 40.

mistakenly believed they had "something worth defending."[53]

Day's entry was followed by Ericka Huggins' contribution to the symposium. Huggins was a director of the Intercommunal Youth Institute, a model school for black and poor youth in East Oakland, California. "We must stop busing children from one bad situation to another and deal with the real problem," she asserted, which, she believed, demanded "a complete overhaul of public education" that put children at the center of the endeavor, rather than treating students "as pawns in a game of political chess."[54]

Huggins' entry was followed by a contribution to the symposium provided by Edgar Friedenberg, who was author of *Coming*

---

[53] Noel Day, "Busing: A Symposium," *Ramparts Magazine*, December 1974, p. 41.

[54] Ericka Huggins, "Busing: A Symposium," *Ramparts Magazine*, December 1974, p. 42.

of Age in America (1965) and a professor at Dalhousie University in Halifax, Nova Scotia, Canada. He seconded Fulwood's, Huggins', and Kohl's assertions that children should have some agency in the events happening to them, especially if those events were traumatic. "Children are people," Friedenberg declared, and as such they deserved the basic human rights and agency afforded to grown folks.[55]

The next article in the symposium was provided by Malecai Andrews, who was a professor of kinesiology at California State University at Hayward and the co-author of *Black Language* (1973). He agreed with Fulwood's assertion that integration was a means and method of trying to make black folks more like the supposedly culturally superior white folks as a means of crafting equality, which, he pointed out was in fact the

---

[55] Edgar Friedenberg, "Busing: A Symposium," *Ramparts Magazine*, December 1974, p. 43.

antithesis of genuine equality. "What if I don't want to be a melted down, diluted version of whitey?" Andrews rhetorically asked readers. Blacks, he elaborated, already knew white culture. It was, he concluded, black culture that black kids "needed some tutoring in."[56]

Andrews' entry to the symposium was followed by an article contributed by Miriam Wasserman, who was a teacher and author of *Demystifying Schools: Writings and Experiences* (1974). There was, she explained, no solution to the problem facing American schools apart from solutions to the social crisis of the nation as a whole. "We have to begin to wrest our humanity back from those who prey on us all," she wrote, in order to "truly reform education."[57]

---

[56] Malecai Andrews, "Busing: A Symposium," *Ramparts Magazine*, December 1974, p. 43.

[57] Miriam Wasserman, "Busing: A Symposium," *Ramparts Magazine*, December 1974, p. 43.

The final contribution to the "Busing: A Symposium" series was written by Jonathan Kozol, who was the author of *Free Schools* (1972). He advocated the Free School program in which he had been actively engaged in the previous eight years. He argued that schools should be small, decentralized, and localized even if it made them vulnerable to appropriation by special interest groups and should offer a child-centered, open structured, individualized, and unoppressive educational experience for all kids. He regretted that the American education system sought to prepare children to earn livings in a corrupt and white supremacist imperial system rather than teaching them to think critically about how to confront the inevitable and inveterate oppression in the social system of which they were made into militarists and corporatist consumers.

Ramparts coverage of the American civil rights movement of the 1960s and 1970s is somewhat typical to mainstream publications in the sense that the publication expressed a great deal of optimism in the early to mid-1960s. However, the magazine's coverage of the civil rights movement was somewhat atypical in the sense that it did not portray the civil rights movement to have concluded after the passage of the Civil Rights and Voting Rights Acts. *Ramparts* also quite rightly connected the Vietnam War, colonialism, imperialism, and the inveterate white supremacy that civil rights activists battled. Rather than being a glorious chapter in which America genuinely absolved its original sin of racism, *Ramparts* depicted the civil rights movement as an ongoing and ever-evolving conflict that demanded constant vigilance. The rise of the prison industrial complex in the late-1960s and early 1970s was as much a reaction to black militancy as it was to a need for more law and order. In short, neither white supremacy in American society nor the necessity of a civil rights movement was ever really achieved or transcended. In short, the issues and dilemmas that grew out of the American Civil War through the modern civil rights movement in postwar America remained largely unresolved well into the twenty-first century. And although the Vietnam War ended and *Ramparts* went out of business in 1975, the need for a robust civil rights movement did not subside in the U.S.

CHAPTER FIVE

"Women's Liberation"

The women's liberation movement was a political alignment of women and feminist intellectualism that emerged in the late 1960s, primarily in the industrialized nations of the Western world. The WLM branch of Radical feminism, based in contemporary philosophy, comprised women of racially- and culturally-diverse backgrounds who proposed that economic, psychological, and social freedom were necessary for women to progress from being second-class citizens in their societies.

Ramparts Magazine published several articles focused on exposing inveterate sexism and misogyny embedded in American society. The first essay *Ramparts* published that overtly criticized American gender norms was published in April 1965. It was titled "Barbie and Her Friends." It was contributed by Donovan Bess, who was a frequent contributor to *The Nation, Harper's*, and other periodicals. Bess half-jokingly described the pernicious cultural importance of the Barbie doll in American society. Barbie was in 1965 a new toy on the market and, as Bess put it, "wildly popular" with little girls. "If America's little girls had access to narcotics," she quipped, they would, no doubt, "give each other injections to escape from the horror of their daily lives." A corporation headquartered at Hawthorne, in Southern California, Bess regretfully explained, directed the fantasies of

American girls as they played. These fantasies seemed, to Bess, to remove the children from little girlhood and transport her into "a teenage Utopia." In 1965 alone, Bess added, about six million American girls regularly played Barbie and thus fantasized about being a teenage party girl. But Barbie was not, Bess wrote, "the kind of young woman you would want to hug (unless one was a GI just coming back from a year in the Aleutians)."[58]

Bess described Barbie as "a frigid-looking teenager" who somehow, through the magic eyes of childhood, was able to simultaneously be a sorority girl, a bride, a career girl, a debutante, and an all-around Superwoman. Little girls, in short, grew up with Mattel-made expectations. By earnestly playing with Barbie and her associates, America's little girls, Bess wrote, learned how

---

[58] Donovan Bess, "Barbie and Her Friends," *Ramparts Magazine*, April 1965, p. 25.

to live in the future. And in the process of playing, the little girls were educated by the promotion department of the Mattel Corporation, the parent Barbie company, which originally hit "big toy-time" with guns. The period of which President John Kennedy sent 16,000 military advisors to South Vietnam (1962-63), Mattel's gross sales volume was $78,030,661 – an increase of fifty-eight percent over the previous year. The corporation also spent more than $9,000,000 in 1964 on advertising and promotion.

"This country is going to need psychiatrists with the experience to treat the coming rash of compound mental fractures (schizophrenia barbiekenia)," Bess wrote.[59] Psychiatrists in fact reported that Barbie-instigated problems already "harassed therapists." So much, Bess added, for the little girls who, in the decade from 1974 to 1984,

---

[59] Ibid, p. 30.

were being equipped to take over the country. A solution to the quandary, the essayist concluded, might be found in the work of Remco Industries, Inc., in Harrison, New Jersey, which had developed a doll called "GI Joe" — America's Movable Fighting Man!" After some hours of sincere play with GI Joe, Bess sardonically concluded, "your boy might well become more impolite, hateful, sadistic and sub-humanly mean than he now is." GI Joe was, Bess joked, "the kind of guy who would love to crash one of Barbie's garden parties."[60]

More than two years passed between Bess' article about Barbie before *Ramparts* published another essay specifically related to women's liberation. The essay was written by two men, Gene Marine and Art Goldberg. It was titled "Abortion Reform: A Big Step Forward? No." In it they described the "world of illegal abortion" as a dirty, degrading,

---

[60] Ibid, p. 30.

frightening, and an unhealthy endeavor in which women sometimes died burning themselves from the inside out with Lysol and from having their uteri torn up with coat hangers. It was a world that existed, Marine and Goldberg wrote, partly because theologians disagreed about the moment at which the soul entered the body—a disagreement that brought misery every year to hundreds of thousands of women who may not have themselves even believed in the existence of a god.

Marine and Goldberg described the American Law Institute's penal code, which, as they described it, "cooked up" by the Institute in 1959. This penal code stipulated that the only legal excuse for abortion in America was to save the life of the mother, or (in Alabama, New Mexico, Oregon and the District of Columbia) to prevent serious and permanent damage to the mother's health. Activist physicians were, however, the essayist explained, increasingly challenging this stipulation in their own private practices.

The American Law Institute thus eventually devised a compromise in the form of a new bill, which would permit abortion (performed in a hospital by a doctor) if the pregnancy would otherwise kill the mother; would seriously and permanently endanger her physical or mental health; or would result in the birth of a child with grave and permanent physical deformity or, as Marine and Goldberg put it, mental retardation. The bill would also allow abortion in the case of a young girl (under the age of 16) or when a pregnancy had resulted from rape or incest. Also, according to abortion reform advocates (who were mostly middle class), it made a neat loophole ("physical or mental health of the mother") through which a determined psychiatrist could "drive a truck."[61]

---

[61] Gene Marine and Art Goldberg, "Abortion Reform: A Big Step Forward? No," *Ramparts Magazine*, July 1967, p. 46.

At the time this essay was published, *Ramparts* was still officially a Catholic publication. That, however, did not stop Goldberg and Marine from lambasting the Roman Catholic Church for derailing abortion reform as they gradually steered the magazine away from the Church and towards the counterculture and Women's Liberation Movement advocacy, both of which were in many ways an afront to the conservatism represented by the Church.

The Roman Catholic Church, the essayists bluntly stated, was "going to see to it that American women" continued to die as a result of being "torn apart by coat hangers or knitting needles."[62] The physicians who so often made public their anguish over the misery caused by America's archaic laws — laws made, incidentally, by men at a time when women were considered little more than

---

[62] Ibid, p. 49.

chattel—could, Goldberg and Marine declared, simply defy the archaic laws and all start performing abortions, which the essayists advocated. "They can't all be put in jail," Marine and Goldberg added. "But the doctors won't do that," the essayists lamented.[63] It, however, should have been obvious to any legislator—and it probably was— Marine and Goldberg asserted, that a woman had a right to determine the use of her own body and to decide her own religious convictions, if any, and about her reproductive rights. But the legislators who had the power to decide, the essayists pessimistically concluded, were no more famous for their courage than the doctors who refused to perform abortions.

In February 1968, nearly six years after the magazine was founded, *Ramparts* finally published an essay about feminism written by a woman (along with her husband, who was

---

[63] Ibid, p. 49.

the managing editor of the publication). The essay was a short social history of the modern Women's Liberation Movement. It was written by Marianne and Warren Hinckle and titled "Women Power: A History of the Rise of the Unusual Movement for Women Power in the United States 1961-1968." The essay chronicled, in part, a who's who of what the Hinckles referred to as the "contemporary women power" movement, which included luminaries such as Joy Kennedy, Betty Friedan, Ruby Dee, Leslie Parrish, Mia Aurbakken Adjali, Florynce Kennedy (no relation to Joy), Viveca Lindfors, Vivian Hallinan, Anne Scheer, and Marilyn Webb, all of whom comprised what the Hinckles referred to as the "irrepressible ladies of the Jeannette Rankin Brigade," an organization of activists named after the legendary suffragette.[64] In the 1960s and 1970s,

---

[64] Warren Hinckle and Marianne Hinckle, "Women Power: A History of the Rise of the Unusual Movement for Women Power in the United States 1961-1968," *Ramparts Magazine*, February 1968, p. 22.

a new generation of pacifists, feminists, and civil rights advocates discovered new inspiration in Rankin, who was a legendary suffragette and the first American woman elected to the House of Representatives (1916, Montana).

The movement to end America's war in Indochina particularly mobilized and galvanized Rankin, who in turn helped inspire many of the luminaries associated with second wave feminism. In January 1968, the Jeannette Rankin Brigade, a coalition of women's peace groups, organized an anti-war march in Washington, D.C. — the largest march by women since the Women Suffrage Parade of 1913. In it Rankin led five thousand participants from Union Station to the steps of the Capitol Building, where they presented a peace petition to House Speaker John McCormack.

A splinter group of activists from the Women's Liberation Movement created a protest within the Brigade's protest by staging a "Burial of True Womanhood" (which Barbie supposedly represented) at Arlington National Cemetery in order to draw attention to the passive role allotted to women as wives and mothers in Cold War American society. The Rankin Brigade had, the Hinckles explained, forged an unparalleled antiwar popular front of women who might normally think twice before even sharing a cab in the rain.

The most unexpected sponsor of all was, the Hinckles asserted, social scientist Betty Friedan, the author of *The Feminine Mystique* (1963), whose antipathy to women's organizations was, the Hinckles derided, "so zealous that it seemed to stem from a secret blood oath rather than a process of intellect."[65] The essayists quoted Friedan as saying that she

---

[65] Ibid, p. 23.

agreed only "reluctantly" to become a sponsor because of the urgent need for protest. Part of the "sexual ideology" Friedan propagated was that she was against sexual discrimination in the peace movement (and anywhere else). Friedan's own group, the National Organization of Women (NOW), was helping to provide equal career opportunities for women, and she was against the war. The Hinckles were, however, critical of Friedan for essentially accepting capitalism and its power structure as presently constituted, noting that Friedan simply wanted some of the men to move over a little to make room for the ladies who were on the back of the bus. This view, the Hinckles explained, put her in the right wing of the new women power movement. In other words, capitalism was, the Hinckles believed, the most significant impediment to women's liberation. And unless capitalism was toppled, they concluded, there would never really be any significant progress in terms of economic, political, and social equality for the women of the world.

In May 1969, *Ramparts* published another article written by Art Goldberg titled "The Perils of the Pill" In it he chronicled birth control activist William Baird. In 1967, Baird gave a lecture to fifteen hundred eager people at Boston University. His topic was birth control. During the course of his talk, he held up a birth control pill for his predominantly white student audience to see. Later, he handed a female student a can of Emko contraceptive foam.

As a result of these two acts, Baird was arrested almost as soon as he had stepped off the stage and was charged with "crimes against chastity." Massachusetts law prohibited disseminating any birth control information, and giving away or exhibiting any drug or article whatever for the prevention of conception, unless it was a physician giving these items to his patient who also had to be married. In October 1967, Baird was convicted for distributing birth control information to unwed women. He thus faced ten years in jail (five for the pill and five for the foam) at the time the essay was published in May 1969.

Baird appealed to the Massachusetts Supreme Court in December 1968; Goldberg anxiously awaited the decision, noting that not even Baird was optimistic. A majority of the Supreme Court justices were, Goldberg explained, between sixty and seventy-five years old white men, and a majority were also Catholic. Baird had also had terrible difficulty getting a lawyer to represent him. The Massachusetts Civil Liberties Union, which at first rushed to involve itself in such an obvious civil liberties test, later mysteriously backed off. Planned Parenthood, a "respectable" birth control organization with a $12 million annual budget at its disposal, and which disliked Baird's confrontations with the law, "bad-mouthed him" in the mainstream press. Many of the speaking engagements Baird relied on to feed his wife and four children were also abruptly and mysteriously canceled. One of the few places that was not frightened off was Harvard University, which invited him to participate in its Distinguished Lecturer Series.

Goldberg explained that Baird was recognized as an authority on birth control in the state of New York and was considered to be a distinguished lecturer by Harvard, but was a convicted felon in the rest of Massachusetts. Baird was aware, Goldberg explained, that if he won his Massachusetts case, it would go a long way towards knocking out many of the so called "fornication laws" that discriminated against unmarried people. If Baird had his way, Goldberg noted, birth control devices would be available to all girls over the age of thirteen, and they would be available in supermarkets as well as drugstores.

Baird had persuaded a Massachusetts legislator to introduce such a bill in the state assembly, but it had not gotten very far. To those who criticized his, as Goldberg put it, "crusade," Baird reflexively cited a Department of Health, Education and Welfare (HEW) statistic that explained that five thousand babies were born to girls under fourteen years of age in 1967 alone. Baird would also tell critics about the girl who came to see him after she had been thrown down a flight of stairs in an attempt to induce a miscarriage and save the family "honor," or those who had tried to abort themselves with knitting needles, straws, coat hangers, Clorox and turpentine.[66]

Baird's appeal of his conviction finally culminated in the 1972 Supreme Court decision *Eisenstadt v. Baird,* which established the right

---

[66] Art Goldberg, "The Perils of the Pill," *Ramparts Magazine,* May 1969, p. 48.

of unmarried persons to possess contraception on the same basis as married couples. The ruling was among the most influential in the U.S. during the entire century by any manner or means of measurement because it enshrined a citizen's right to be free from unwarranted governmental intrusion into matters so fundamentally affecting a person as to whether to bear or beget a child, which paved the way for the passage of *Roe v. Wade* (1973).

In December 1969, *Ramparts* published an article titled "The Rise of Women's Liberation," written by Marlene Dixon, who was a professor of sociology at McGill University and an activist in the Women's Liberation Movement. Professor Dixon described the 1960s as an era of liberation and explained that women had been swept up by that ferment along with African Americans, Latin Americans, American Indians and poor whites, what Dixon described as "the whole soft underbelly of this society."[67]

She described the base of the women's liberation movement as encompassing poor black and poor white women on relief, working women exploited in the labor force, middle class women "incarcerated" in the split-level dream house, college girls awakening to the fact that sexiness was not the crowning achievement in life, and movement women who had discovered that in a freedom movement they themselves were not free. In less than four years women had, Dixon explained, created a variety of organizations, from the nationally-based middle class National Organization of Women to local radical feminist groups in every major city in North America. This new movement included caucuses within nearly every New Left group

---

[67] Marlene Dixon, "The Rise of Women's Liberation," *Ramparts Magazine*, December 1969, p. 57.

and within most professional associations in the social sciences. Ranging in politics from reform to revolution, it had produced critiques of almost every segment of American society and constructed an ideology that rejected every hallowed cultural assumption about the nature and role of women.

In 1968, Dixon noted, the movement stressed male chauvinism and psychological oppression. But in 1969, she elaborated, the emphasis was on understanding the economic and social roots of women's oppression, and the analyses ranged from social democracy to Marxism.[68] But the most striking change of all, she argued, had been the loss of fear. Women were, she asserted, no longer afraid that their rebellion would threaten their very identity as women. They were, she asserted, no longer frightened by their own militancy, "but

---

[68] Ibid, p. 58.

liberated by it." Women's Liberation was, in short, an idea whose time had come.[69]

She described marriage as the chief vehicle for the perpetuation of the oppression of women; it was, she argued, through the role of wife that the subjugation of women was maintained. In a very real way the role of wife had been, she declared, the genesis of women's rebellion throughout history. A woman was first defined by the man to whom she was attached, but more particularly by the man she married, and secondly by the children she raised—hence the anxiety over sexual attractiveness, and the "frantic scramble" for boyfriends and husbands. Having obtained and married a man the race was then on to have children, in order that their attractiveness and accomplishments might add more social worth. In a woman, not having children was,

---

[69] Ibid, p. 58.

she explained, seen as an incapacity somewhat akin to impotence in a man.[70]

As such, Dixon believed, radical social change had to occur before there could be significant improvement in the social position of women. Some form of socialism was, she declared, a minimum requirement for liberating women, considering the changes that had to come in the institutions of marriage and the family. The intrinsic radicalism of the struggle for women's liberation thus necessarily linked women with all other oppressed groups. The heart of the movement, as in all freedom movements, rested in women's knowledge, whether articulated or still only an illness without a name, that they were not inferior — "not chicks, nor bunnies, nor quail, nor cows, nor bitches, nor ass, nor meat." Women, she declared, needed to "learn the meaning of rage," the violence that

---

[70] Ibid, p. 60.

liberated "the human spirit." The rhetoric of invective was, she added, an equally essential stage, for in discovering and venting their rage "against the enemy — and the enemy in everyday life was men — women also experienced the justice of their own violence..." Women must learn, she concluded, "to know themselves as revolutionaries" and "become hard and strong in their determination, while retaining their humanity and tenderness."[71]

In June 1970, *Ramparts* published an essay titled "Women and the Myth of Consumerism," contributed by Ellen Willis, who was an activist in the Women's Liberation Movement in Colorado. She argued that if white radicals were really serious about revolution, they were going to have to "discard

---

[71] Ibid, p. 63.

a lot of bullshit ideology created by and for educated white middle-class males."[72]

A good example of what had to be discarded if women were to ever be truly free, she asserted, was the popular theory of consumerism. The theory was, she noted, alleged to be particularly applicable to women, for women did most of the actual buying. Their consumption was, however, she argued, often directly related to their oppression (i.e. makeup, soap flakes, et cetera), and they were a special target of advertisers, who were mostly men. According to this view, capitalist society defined women as consumers, and the purpose of the prevailing media image of women as passive sexual objects was to sell products. It thus followed that the beneficiaries of this depreciation of women were not men but the corporate power structure. Although

---

[72] Ellen Willis, "Women and the Myth of Consumerism," *Ramparts Magazine*, June 1970, p. 13.

the consumerism theory had, through the 1950s and 1960s, taken on the invulnerability of religious dogma, like most dogmas its basic function was, Willis argued, to defend the interests of its adherents—in this case, the class, sexual and racial privileges of Movement people.

She noted that there was nothing inherently wrong with consumption. Shopping and consuming were, she conceded enjoyable human activities and the marketplace had been a center of social life for thousands of years. But the profit system that fueled consumerism was, she argued, "patently oppressive," not only because relatively trivial luxuries were available, but because basic necessities were not. The locus of the oppression thus resided in the production function: people had no control over which commodities were produced (or services performed), in what amounts, under what conditions, or how these commodities were distributed. Corporations, she pointed out, made these decisions and based them solely on their profit potential.[73]

It was thus, she added, more profitable to produce luxuries for the affluent (or for that matter for the poor, on exploitative installment plans) than to produce and make available food, housing, medical care, education, and recreational and cultural facilities according to the needs and desires of the people. As this system was, the profusion of commodities was, in Willis' mind, a genuine and powerful "compensation for oppression." Under present conditions, she wrote, people were preoccupied with consumer goods not because brainwashing, but because buying was "the one pleasurable activity not only permitted but actively encouraged by our rulers."[74]

The pleasure of eating an ice cream cone may be, she noted, minor compared to the

---

[73] Ibid.
[74] Ibid, p. 14.

pleasure of meaningful, autonomous work, but the former was easily available and the latter was not. And the objectification of women in advertisements, she argued, reflected women as they were conditioned by men in a sexist society to behave. Male supremacy was, she added, the oldest and most basic form of class exploitation; and it was not invented by a smart ad man. "The real evil of the media image of women," she wrote, was that it supported "the sexist status quo" that had existed since time immemorial.[75]

Willis then explained that fashion, cosmetics and feminine hygiene ads were actually aimed more at men – the breadwinners – than at women. These ads, she explained, encouraged men to expect women to sport all the latest trappings of what she referred to as "sexual slavery." That advertisers exploited women's subordination

---

[75] Ibid, p. 15.

rather than caused it could be clearly seen, she believed, because male fashions and toiletries had also become big business.

Willis also asserted that consumerism for women was actually work. In other words, conforming to the object that men had thrust upon women was a woman's job, whether she was conscious of it or not; clothes and make up were tools of the trade. Consumerism as applied to women was thus, she asserted, blatantly sexist. The pervasive image of what she referred to as the "empty-headed female consumer constantly trying her husband's patience with her extravagant purchases contributed," Ellis argued, to the myth of male superiority because women were supposedly incapable of spending money rationally.

She further postulated that there was an analogous racial stereotype to the notion that all women wanted was a new product to appease them—like "the black with his

Cadillac and his magenta shirts," she wrote.[76] She further noted that the consumerism line allowed Movement men to avoid recognizing that they also exploited women by attributing women's oppression solely to capitalism, which fit neatly into an already existing radical theory and concern, saving the Movement the trouble of tackling the real problems of women's liberation. If, however, she wrote, the New Left was truly willing to build a mass movement it was imperative to recognize that no individual decision, like rejecting consumption, could liberate people. "We must stop arguing about whose lifestyle is better (and secretly believing ours is)" she concluded, "and tend to the task of collectively fighting our own oppression and the ways in which we oppress others. If members of the New Left were to create a political alternative to sexism,

---

[76] Ibid, p 16.

racism and capitalism, she concluded, the consumer problem would take care of itself.[77]

In June 1970, *Ramparts* published an essay titled "Off the Pill?" written by Judith Coburn, who was a journalist and a member of Washington, D.C. Women's Liberation. Her essay detailed the lives of thirty members of her organization, which had disrupted Senator Gaylord Nelson's hearings on the Birth Control Pill. The group went to the hearings to protest the panel comprised of representatives from drug companies, population control experts, and the government, all of whom were men.

These men had, Coburn believed, given the Pill a clean bill of health at women's expense. The protest she took part was, she wrote, a particular shock to Senator Nelson—a longtime foe of the drug industry—who held the hearings for what he believed to be women's best interests. But congressional

---

[77] Ibid, p. 16.

hearings, especially those dominated by male senators, doctors, and drug researchers—could not, she argued, possibly deal with women's terrible dilemma about the Pill.

This dilemma was, Coburn explained, a kind of catch-22 that presented women with two bad options: 1. Should women take the Pill, chancing dangerous side effects including stroke and/or death? or 2. should women risk what doctors and population control experts portrayed as certain pregnancy? The issue had thus, Coburn lamented, been reduced to haggling over the content of a proposed Food and Drug Administration warning to be put in Pill packages.

In March 1970, Coburn and members of Women's Liberation of Washington D.C. staged a sit-in in the Department of Health, Education, and Welfare Secretary Robert Finch's office in the hopes of establishing the right of women to control their own medical and personal lives. Word had, Coburn explained, gone out quietly from the Department of Health, Education and Welfare that the Pill warning was to be watered down in order to protect the interests of physicians who feared that they could be retroactively charged with malpractice suits for prescribing a medication with a 700-word warning of side effects, which had been reduced to a 30-word warning. Women had not, Coburn noted, been involved at all in the preparation of the original statement or in its revision.[78]

As the Nelson hearings made clear, there was no immediate solution to what Coburn referred to as the women's birth control dilemma. Many women, she explained, believed that the best alternatives to the Pill, which many felt was unsafe, were existing forms of contraception backed up by freely available abortions. This would, Coburn believed, provide neither the convenience nor

---

[78] Judith Coburn, "Off the Pill?" *Ramparts Magazine*, June 1970, p. 49.

the psychological liberation of the Pill, but it would provide freedom from fear of unwanted pregnancy. Even where abortion laws were repealed or liberalized at the state level, she added, women often had to depend on male doctors—many of whom refused—to perform what she referred to as "the simple operation."[79]

Women's health needs were, she argued, profoundly political rights. It was thus up to women to decide what form of contraceptive to use, and whether to have abortions. Women themselves, she wrote, must decide whether or not to take the Pill, and whether or not to have children. If the population control movement was, she added, serious about limiting children, it should think about fighting to change society so that women could choose careers other than those of housewife and mother. For married women this meant around-the-clock day-care centers at

---

[79] Ibid, p. 49.

their place of work. For men it meant sharing equally with women the responsibilities of children, household and contraception. For all women, she concluded, it meant redefining their lives and medical needs through political struggle and their own personal liberation. It meant, in short, learning that the sexual revolution did not really have much at all to do with the Pill.

In August 1970, *Ramparts* published an article contributed by Lucinda Cisler titled "Abortion Reform: The New Tokenism." Cisler had been active in women's liberation since 1968 and was the author of *Women: A Bibliography* (1970). She was also the president of New Yorkers for Abortion Law Repeal, which opposed the passage of New York's amended abortion law for the reasons she set forth in her article. These amendments included:

1. Abortions may only be performed in licensed hospitals.

2. Abortions may only be performed by licensed physicians.
3. Abortions may not be performed beyond a certain time in pregnancy, unless the woman's life was at stake.
4. Abortions may only be performed when the married woman's husband or the young single woman's parents gave their consent.

The most important thing feminists had done and needed to keep doing, Cisler believed, was to insist that the basic reason for repealing the laws and making abortions available was "justice," which she defined as the right to have an abortion.[80] Because no one else except the women's movement was going to cry out against these restrictions, she concluded, it was up to feminists to make the strongest and most

---

[80] Lucinda Cisler, "Abortion Reform: The New Tokenism [I] Abortion Law Repeal (sort of): A Warning to Women," *Ramparts Magazine*, August 1970, p. 19.

precise demands upon the lawmakers— who "ostensibly existed to serve the rights of American women."[81]

In September 1970, *Ramparts* published an excerpt from *La Vieillesse* (1970) titled "On Aging," which was contributed by Simone de Beauvoir, the French writer, intellectual, existentialist philosopher, political activist, feminist, and social theorist perhaps best known for her seminal book, *The Second Sex* (1949). Though a legendary feminist critical theorist, her essay in the September 1970 edition of *Ramparts* focused mostly on the rights of the elderly.

"Society concerns itself with the individual only insofar as he is productive," de Beauvoir wrote, lamenting the indignity thrust upon the elderly in Western Society. Her essay traced the oppression of the elderly in Western Civilization primarily to capitalism, which

---

[81] Ibid, p. 21.

viewed those unable to earn money, such as housewives and the elderly, as public charges and a drain on the Gross Domestic Product of a nation. "Once one has understood what the condition of old people is," she wrote, "one cannot be content to demand more generous 'politics of old age,' higher pensions, decent housing, organized leisure activities." It was, she declared, the whole system, which was at stake, and thus the demand could only be a radical one: "to change life." The ideal society she envisioned was one in which old age, like sexism and misogyny, were transcended in the name of genuine justice, which, she believed, simply did not jive with capitalism.[82]

In May 1971, *Ramparts* published an interview of Anaïs Nin conducted by Judy Oringer. Nin was a French-American diarist, essayist, novelist, and writer of short stories

---

[82] Simone de Beauvoir, "On Aging," *Ramparts Magazine*, September 1970, p. 25.

and erotica. Born to Cuban parents in France, she was the daughter of composer Joaquín Nin and Rosa Culmell, a classically trained singer. Nin spent the early years of her life in Spain and Cuba, about sixteen years in Paris, and the remaining half of her life in the U.S., where she became an established author.

The explosion of the feminist movement in the late-1960s and early 1970s fostered new feminist perspectives on Nin's writings, which made her a popular lecturer at various universities. "We need heroines to illumine the way," she told Oringer, "to stir up our courage."[83] Nin, however, expressed trepidation about the trajectory of the more militant women's liberation advocates. "I do not believe in war against men any more than I believe in war against other countries," she explained to Oringer. "We can only liberate

---

[83] Judy Oringer, "Anais Nin on Women," *Ramparts Magazine*, May 1971, p. 44.

ourselves by joint efforts… To change from love of man to love of woman is not going to solve the conflicts of relationship."[84]

She elaborated that she harbored "no faith in political systems or outer changes" noting that the U.S. was still at war and so she decided to concentrate her faith on inner changes that in turn influenced others, ultimately, she explained, radiating into the community. The success of collective action, she believed, depended on the quality of individual contribution. She added that she would like women to become more aware of their individual situation and personal problems before they rushed into blind collective action. She also believed that a lot of women's liberation actions were a waste of effort and energy. It was, she argued, negative action to attack the male writers who did not understand or portray women adequately. It

---

[84] Ibid, p. 44.

would be more positive, she noted, to study women writers who had struggled to establish their own patterns. "When I changed," she said, "it changed the world around me, it changed the men around me. Not by aggression and hostility but by relationship and exchange of feeling and thought."[85]

Oringer's interview with Nin was followed in the May 1971 edition or *Ramparts* by an essay titled "The Aesthetics of Childbirth," contributed by Lindsy Van Gelder. She explained that a traumatic experience in childbirth was just the first taste of the "oppressive conditions a woman faced when she decided (or did not decide—for in most places she could not get a legal abortion) to have a child." There remained, she noted, the question of day care, the problem of raising a child outside the limitations of the nuclear family, the day-to-day grind of diapers and

---

[85] Ibid, p. 44.

"Mad Housewifery" — not to mention the enormous task of bringing up sons and daughters who would not be crippled by the sexual stereotyping that was part and parcel of what she perceived to be "all the other problems" society suffered in the early 1970s.

Sexism, she wrote, began in the womb, when everyone assumed that, of course, "you want a boy."[86] At birth, she regretted, girl babies were wrapped in pink blankets and boys in blue, the sexism of which Dr. Benjamin Spock, she lamented, believed was good for children. The fight for educated childbirth, Van Gelder argued, was a crucial one. She added that the suffragists who saw their salvation in chloroform were on to something basic: women were defined by, and oppressed by, society's idea of what actually happened in women's wombs. Little girls with ringlets and paper dolls grew up into women who felt

---

[86] Lindsy Van Gelder, "The Aesthetics of Childbirth," *Ramparts Magazine*, May 1971, p. 51.

embarrassed buying Tampax in the drug store. It was, however, high time, Van Gelder concluded, "to demystify the womb and spread the word: Woman is Beautiful."[87]

In September 1971, *Ramparts* published an essay titled "Rape: The All-American Crime," contributed by Susan Griffin, who was a feminist poet working on a trilogy of novellas examining the psychic life of women. She noted that according to estimates by independent criminologists, rape was the most frequently committed violent crime in the U.S. in the early 1970s. She described rape as a form of "mass terrorism," for, she explained, the victims of rape were chosen indiscriminately, but the propagandists for male supremacy broadcast that it was women who caused rape by being unchaste or in the wrong place at the

---

[87] Ibid, p. 51.

wrong time—in essence, by "behaving as though they were free."[88]

She noted how the threat of rape was a poignant impediment to women's liberation. The fear of rape kept women off the streets at night, kept women at home, and kept women passive and modest for fear that they be thought provocative. It was, she explained, part of human dignity to be able to defend oneself, and women thus were learning to defend themselves. Some women. She noted, had learned karate; some to shoot guns.

And yet, she lamented, women would not truly be free until the threat of rape and the atmosphere of violence was ended, and to end that the nature of male behavior had to fundamentally change. But rape was not, she explained, an isolated act that could be rooted

---

[88] Susan Griffin, "Rape: The All-American Crime," *Ramparts Magazine*, September 1971, p. 35.

out from patriarchy without ending patriarchy itself. The same men and power structure that victimized women were, she wrote, "engaged in the act of raping Vietnam, raping Black people, and the very earth we live upon." Rape was, she added, a classic act of domination in which emotions of hatred, contempt, and the desire to break or violate personality took place. She believed that this "breaking of the personality" characterized modern life itself. No simple reform could thus, she believed, eliminate rape. As the symbolic expression of the white male hierarchy, rape was, she concluded, the "quintessential act of American civilization."[89]

In October 1971, *Ramparts* published a review of Vivian Gornick and Barbara R. Moran's *Woman in Sexist Society: Studies in Power and Powerlessness* (1971), contributed by Roberta Salper, who was an Associate

---

[89] Ibid, p. 35.

Professor of Humanities at SUNY at Old Westbury and the author of *Female Liberation: History and Current Politics* (1971). Gornick and Moran, Salper explained, placed women alongside the prototypical Wandering Jew and Noble Savage, "symbolically beyond the pale of ordinary human existence." Such a vantage point, Salper argued, not only provided valuable perspective for critiquing society, it also, she asserted, encouraged the camaraderie of the outsider that allowed Gornick and Moran to write sympathetically about all marginalized groups. Gornick and Moran, Salper added, also attacked the anti-female culture created by a patriarchal society that stratified people by sex, class and race, and defined woman "not by the struggling development of her brain or her will or her spirit, but rather by her child-bearing properties and her status as companion to men who make, and do, and rule the earth."[90]

Woman in Sexist Society was comprised of thirty essays that explored multifarious aspects of sexism and was divided into four parts — I. Beauty, Love and Marriage: The Myth and the Reality; II. Woman is Made, Not Born; III. Woman at Work; and IV. Social Issues and Feminism: Education, Homosexuality, Race and Radicalism — which served as categories for the examination of the role and image of women in literature, history, the creative arts, the social sciences, the business world, sexual relationships, and educational philosophy. The breadth and depth of the text made it, Salper concluded, an important book that members of the New Left, especially those active in the

---

[90] Roberta Salper, "review of Vivian Gornick and Barbara R. Moran's *Woman in Sexist Society: Studies in Power and Powerlessness*," *Ramparts Magazine*, October 1971, p. 64

Women's Liberation Movement, were highly advised to read.

In December 1971, *Ramparts* published a lengthy essay titled "Carnal Knowledge: A Portrait of Four Hookers," contributed by Kate Coleman. Her account of the trials and tribulations of four prostitutes in New York City had a distinctly Marxist tone. Coleman, for example, examined portrayed these women as legitimate laborers who plied a trade that had existed for thousands of years. Coleman also avoided a moral critique of their profession. "To be sure," she wrote, "hookers all over the world are economic and sociological victims;" but she felt this view to be too one-dimensional for a situation in a country of plenty."[91] In other words, she perceived prostitutes to be inevitable victims of a rapacious capitalist system.

---

[91] Kate Coleman, "Carnal Knowledge: A Portrait of Four Hookers," *Ramparts Magazine*, December 1971, p. 16.

Talking with call girls in Manhattan also quickly dispelled Coleman's illusions that high-earning call girls were able to afford liberation. As Coleman's conversations with her case studies unfolded, it soon became apparent to her that high-class hookers were exploited as rigorously (if more subtly) as any streetwalker was. There was, Coleman noted, no job security — certainly no job protection, pensions, or other fringe benefits. Other hazards included a high rate of venereal disease as well as danger from clients who may be "psychopaths."

Moreover, Coleman argued, a hooker's self-image as a woman suffered from the worst female stereotypes: "submissive, in need of male protection, a heavy preoccupation with material goods, fit only for a fuck." The stigma of prostitution also, Coleman explained, reinforced this image by confining most hookers to the very narrow social milieu of other hookers, pimps and general "criminal" types. Hookers were also "at the mercy" of masculine overlords, most notably pimps and johns. Male police and male judges also arrested the women and sentenced them to prison; and male legislators made the laws that condemned call girls.[92]

Most often, Coleman wrote, it was a prostitute's economic dilemma coupled with the psychologically damaging belief that they were not fit for anything else that kept them in prostitution and unconscious of how they were exploited. Some of the women Coleman interviewed honestly believed prostitution offered them more personal freedom than did working as a nine-to-five drudge in a department store or factory, which, Coleman asserted, was an "eloquent testimony" to the degree to which women actually lacked control over the forces that shaped their opportunities and their lives.[93]

---

[92] Ibid, p. 17.

[93] Ibid, p. 18.

Speaking to the popularity of Gonzo journalism of the early 1970s, Coleman's research for her article included taking pay to sleep with a john, a photographer in his mid-thirties who she admitted to being sexually attracted to. She was also propositioned at Clare's whorehouse in Manhattan by a bespectacled john who she described as "repulsive, flaccid, gross and wearing an American flag pin in his lapel—a complete turn-off."[94] She thus refused to perform sex acts on him. The actual call girls at Clare's were quick to point out to Coleman that they were not permitted to refuse a john's request for sex, no matter how disgusting he might be, which further educated Coleman that working girls were as imprisoned by capitalism as were the housewives described by Betty Friedan in *Feminine Mystique* (1963).

---

[94] Ibid, p. 28.

In December 1971, *Ramparts* published another article written by Roberta Salper titled "Women's Studies." Salper hailed the fact that one hundred colleges and universities offered at least one course on women during the 1970-71 school year—courses such as "The Socialization Process of Women," "Imperialism and its Relation to Sexism," "Education of Women," and "Women in the Labor Force." Women's Studies she wrote, was well on its way to being ushered into the "hallowed groves of academe" and was perceived by publications such as *Newsweek* to be the "hottest new wrinkle in higher education."[95]

The implications of having an "academic arm" of a broader-based political movement were, Professor Salper explained, important to consider because the issue involved the political development of the Women's Liberation Movement, the structure

---

[95] Roberta Salper, "Women's Studies," *Ramparts Magazine*, December 1971, p. 56.

and control of American higher education, and the relationship between the two. And herein lied, she explained, the political potential of Women's Studies: to the extent that the university-based programs could create links with other sectors of society, the traditional divisions — student vs. worker, black vs. white, man vs. woman — used to maintain what she referred to as the "American Way of Life" would inevitably, she believed, be weakened as a result of the popularization of women's studies.

But this was, she rightly warned, going to be no easy task, for on the one hand, the American system of higher education had what she referred to as a "well-greased escape valve" for such "radical emergencies" — the corporate foundation grant.[96] The cultural celebration of sisterhood associated with the rise of women's studies programs on campuses

---

[96] Ibid, p. 56.

across the country could be, she believed, a crucial steppingstone to radical political action, but not, she warned, if culture became a "surrogate for political development," or if the women's liberation movement could not criticize its own illusions.

As such, women who were serious about changing the centers of power in the U.S. should, she asserted, stay in contact with these centers and not opt for the middle-class freedom of stepping out for personal liberation. If the polarization of external and internal co-optation was avoided, she added, Women's Studies Programs had the potential for developing into bases for the acquisition of knowledge and skills and development of "cadres" for the Women's Movement. The next step — the most difficult and crucial one — was, she wrote, linking the university-based programs with other areas in society. That meant forcing the educational institutes to allow sectors outside the university to use and benefit from their resources, and thereby creating what she argued should be the ultimate goal of Women's Studies: a broad-based movement dedicated to creating real social change. Women's Studies, she concluded, should generate not the kind of feminism that culminated in the right to choose between Hubert Humphrey and Richard Nixon, but the kind of feminism whose demands could no longer be granted by American society because they were demands for a socialist, non-sexist, non-racist society.[97]

In the final three months of 1972, *Ramparts* provided a platform to the Women's News Collective, which had grown out of a weekly radio program of Women's News at *KPFA* in Berkeley, California. The WHC welcomed readers' contributions, particularly items from women's struggles outside the U.S. The first essay contributed by the WHC was

---

[97] Ibid, p. 60.

published in October 1972. They asserted that The Bell System, according to Equal Employment Opportunity Commission documents, was the largest oppressor of women workers in the U.S., due in part to the fact that their policies toward women were "morally and ethically indefensible," and since July 2, 1965, they had "been against the law."[98]

The report quantified the difference paid to female employees as $500 million per year less than males with comparable personal characteristics. In regard to blacks, the report found that progress in black employment meant the hiring of large numbers of black females as entry-level operators. According to the report, the company was attempting to comply with racial requirements by substituting another form of low-paid work — in effect, replacing one form of illegal discrimination with another.

---

[98] The Women's News Collective, "Women's News Collective," *Ramparts Magazine*, October 1972, p. 16.

The WHC then turned its sites on the plight of women in London, namely those who cleaned office buildings by night and cared for their children during day. The two male-dominated trade unions that the women were eligible to join, the WHC lamented, failed to support and encourage them in their struggle for better pay and working conditions. Lastly, the essayists turned their attention to the question of the financial worth of housewives, calculating the annual salary at $13,391.56. The twelve job categories the essayists associated with being a housewife included: nursemaid, dietitian, food buyer, cook, dishwasher, housekeeper, laundress, seamstress, practical nurse, maintenance person, gardener and chauffeur. The annual salary of $13,391.56 did not, the WHC noted, even include a price for the toll associated with childbearing.

In November 1972, The Women's News Collective targeted healthcare. They noted that the wages, skills and prestige of doctors in the industry were especially high. But, the essayists added, just ten percent of them in 1972 were women. Despite the very high percentage of men as doctors, seventy-five percent of all health workers in the medical field were women, for, the WHC explained, much health work reflected traditionally "feminine" functions: nurturing, caring, cooking, educating, and cleaning.

The supporting cast of registered and practical nurses, dieticians, technicians, social workers, housekeepers and clerks however found that most jobs were a "dead-end." Such low paying, semi-skilled and unskilled work had traditionally gone to women, especially Third World women. There was thus wage discrimination as well as job discrimination.

For example, female practical nurses made an average of ten dollars per week less than their male colleagues. In only one field were men's and women's salaries equal: medical technology. Throughout the medical system, women could also routinely expect less advancement than men. Yet with their numerical supremacy, the Women's News Collective argued, women health workers represented the potential for a revolution in the industry.

The essayists then pointed out that the divorce rate was increasing to an "incredible degree," noting that The Department of Health, Education and Welfare reported that the rate of divorce was nearing half of the new marriages in a given year. The WHC thus suggested that women considering marriage ought to invest in divorce insurance because if the marriage survived, the policy could be converted into an educational fund for the children, or even into a regular life insurance policy. The WHC concluded the essay by hailing the fact that according to a British security expert, a revolution in organized crime was producing a new variety of women gang leaders and urban guerrillas. Women had, the WHC hailed, taken leading positions as operators and planners in the underworld organizations of Britain, the U.S., Germany, and the Irish Republican Army.

In December 1972, the Women's News Collective argued that the sex of a psychologist may interfere with his or her clinical judgment. After studying thirty experienced, professional psychologists, Dr. Norma Haan and Dr. Norman Livson found that male psychologists quickly picked up such deviations from the "male" norms as passivity and dependency, while females were more apt to notice "male" tendencies such as condescension and excessive concern with power and self-control.

In other words, it was as though male doctors kept a keener eye out for defections from the male stereotype, while women were more alert to the excesses of males in the service of that stereotype. Male psychologists also tended to be more critical of both sexes, while female psychologists tended to be more supportive. Female psychologists also evaluated women more favorably, giving them credit for intellectual competence and self-acceptance, while male doctors frequently accused women of irritability and rebelliousness.

    The WHC then turned their attention to Carolyn Aiello, Elizabeth B. Johnson, Agustina D. Armendariz and Jacqueline Jaramillo. These women had recently charged sexual discrimination and sued the State of California in order to receive pregnancy benefits under the state's temporary disability insurance. Women in California could not collect disability benefits during the term of their pregnancy or for twenty-eight days thereafter, even though they paid into this fund. In addition, women were denied benefits for any condition arising out of pregnancy. This provision affected approximately 200,000 workingwomen in California each year. Male workers, however, were covered for such strictly-male disabilities as hernias, circumcisions, and prostatectomies, and the state even paid benefits to workers who were recovering from sex-change operations. The plaintiffs involved in the suit maintained that they had faced considerable financial hardship and mental strain because of the unequal coverage. Three of the women were, the essayists noted, seriously ill due to complications arising from pregnancy, and one woman had lost her job as a result of her pregnancy.

An essay titled "Bankamerilib: Can Lynda Bird be Liberated?" contributed by Sheila Daar was also published in the December 1972 edition of *Ramparts*. In it Daar chronicled the happenings at the symposium on "Women in the Economy," which was sponsored by *The Ladies Home Journal*, Bank of America, and its subsidiary, BankAmericard.

Earlier in 1972, Bank of America had been criticized by Movement women for discrimination against its female employees. Under the circumstances, the conference promised to provide what Daar referred to as "a curious view" of the Women's Liberation Movement, especially considering that the only "homemaker" to participate in the symposium was the wife of the president of BankAmericard. To anyone who might have been concerned about the fact that women earned only fifty-nine percent as much as men, Daar wrote, or that during the Nixon administration unemployment of women (and minorities) had risen to an all-time post-World War II high, or that three-quarters of all clerical workers and two-thirds of all service workers were women, Nixon's Chairman of the Council of Economic Advisors, Herbert Stein, had a momentous announcement: President Nixon had recently released a statement asking Stein to form an Advisory Committee on the Economic Role of Women. "And thus," Daar sardonically quipped, "an advisory committee to an advisory committee would conduct yet another study of the 'problem.'" Daar ultimately described the symposium on "Women in the Economy" as little more than a publicity stunt and public relations event for Bank of America and the Nixon administration designed to create the image that they were committed to women's liberation while in fact profiting hand-over-fist from white male supremacy of the capitalist system.

In March 1973, *Ramparts* published an essay titled "Cosmopolitan: The Feminine Plastique," written by Robin Reisig, who was a regular contributor to *The Village Voice*. In it she profiled Helen Gurney Brown, who was the editor-in-chief of *Cosmopolitan Magazine*.

Reisig described Brown as "an evangelist" born in Little Rock, Arkansas, who "genuinely wanted all girls to be beautiful and everybody to be charming." Brown was, Reisig wrote, a girl for whom the American Dream had come true. Brown had scrimped and saved and entered beauty contests. She also stayed late at the office, did not take coffee breaks, and she constantly submitted memos. She also capped her teeth and dieted, cleared her acne, fixed her nose, fixed her hair, and went to half a dozen analysts until she found the right one.

Brown was also, Reisig wrote, a quintessential child of the 1950s and *Cosmopolitan*, for all its sexual "liberation" still seemed to belong in some ways to that era when young women still "oozed into makeup and curled into rollers and sweated toward one ultimate goal: landing a man." Brown's dream, Reisig added, was "the biggest, the most dazzling, and she got it all." And every month, Reisig lamented, a million and a half women still pursued the dream of getting the man with the help of Brown's magazine.

Cosmopolitan, Reisig regretted, did not seek to change the basic conditions of the traditional gender supremacy that the

Women's Liberation Movement combated, but operated within them.[99] *Cosmopolitan*, Reisig explained, informed each woman how she could make it with a man, rather than how women could achieve true equality together. Gloria Steinem's as *Ms. Magazine* was, Reisig believed, doing what Cosmopolitan failed to do. *Cosmopolitan* was, Reisig concluded, merely another way for women to cope with oppression by consuming products and by imbibing the pernicious notion that the only way to satisfaction was, even for workingwomen, being with a man.[100]

---

[99] Robin Reisig, "*Cosmopolitan*: The Feminine Plastique," *Ramparts Magazine*, March 1973, p. 54.

[100] *Ms.* is an American liberal feminist magazine co-founded by second-wave feminists and sociopolitical activists Gloria Steinem and Dorothy Pitman Hughes. Founding editors were Letty Cottin Pogrebin, Mary Thom, Patricia Carbine, Joanne Edgar, Nina Finkelstein, and Mary Peacock. *Ms.* first appeared in 1971 as an insert in *New York Magazine*. The first stand-alone issue appeared in January 1972 with funding from New York editor Clay Felker. From July 1972 to 1987, it appeared on a monthly basis. It now publishes quarterly.

In June 1973, *Ramparts* published a review titled "Women's Fiction: Who's Afraid of Virginia Woolf: *The Awakening*, by Kate Chopin," which was contributed by Elizabeth Fishel. In it she reviewed Chopin's *The Awakening* (1899), Tillie Olsen's *Tell Me a Riddle* (1961), and Alix Kate Shulman's *Memoirs of an Ex-Prom Queen* (1972). Chopin's *The Awakening* provided readers with a frank look at a woman's life at the turn of the nineteenth century. The novella shocked critics and audiences alike when it was first published. Many of those who were shocked, Fishel explained, showed little sympathy for the author or her central protagonist, Edna Pontellier.

Olsen's *Tell Me a Riddle* rendered a timely portrait of a working class couple when the gender determined differences in their experiences of poverty and familial life gave rise to bitter conflict after almost four decades of marriage. As she died from cancer, Eva, the protagonist, recollected a revolutionary past that both critiqued and offered hope for women diligently pursuing equal rights.

Memoirs of an Ex-Prom Queen was a sardonic portrayal of one white, middle-class, Midwestern girl's coming-of-age. Shulman's *Memoirs of an Ex-Prom Queen* presented, Fishel believed, a wry and prescient look at a range of experiences treated at the time as taboo but which were ultimately accepted as matters of major political significance by the early 1970s: sexual harassment, job discrimination, the sexual double-standard, rape, abortion restrictions, the double binds of marriage and motherhood, and the frantic quest for beauty. "This could be the beginning of a new era of women's fiction," Fishel concluded, "a potentially revolutionary moment in American literature."[101]

---

[101] Elizabeth Fishel, "Women's Fiction: Who's Afraid of Virginia Woolf: The Awakening, by Kate Chopin," *Ramparts Magazine*, June 1973, p. 48.

In November 1973, *Ramparts* published another essay contributed by Fishel titled "The Women's Self-Help Movement." In it Fishel argued that the first lesson of the Women's Health Movement was to "begin with the personal." All women had what she referred to as "bogeys" of their own and that the energy of the burgeoning Women's Health Movement derived its potential to speak to the needs of all women, regardless of age, race, or economic background. The Women's Self-Help Movement could, Fishel explained, be summed as follows: in the American health care system of the early 1970s, women consumed most of the services but men still had most of the control. Women made, on average, twenty-five percent more visits to the doctor per year than men, some of which were for specifically gynecological reasons; others were mothers' pediatric visits with their children; still others occurred because women had typically been expected to indulge their pains and men to ignore or transcend them. Women also consumed fifty percent more prescription drugs and were admitted to hospitals more frequently than men. Two out of three mental patients were also women.

As workers, women comprised about seventy percent of the health labor force. Still, most patients and health workers remained under the supervision and control of male doctors (only seven percent of American physicians were women and, of these, most specialized in pediatrics). Men also controlled hospitals, lead medical research, and headed drug companies. These professionals of what Fishel referred to as the "Medical-Industrial Complex" were, she believed, generally more preoccupied with the health of their profits than with the health of the people they supposedly served.

Such was, Fishel explained, the stuff out of which movements were made, and in 1973 the Women's Health Movement had emerged as a nation-wide force. The Movement's de facto manifesto, *Our Bodies, Our Selves* (1973) was originally put together by the Boston Women's Health Collective as a series of discussion papers that explored everything from virginity through prepared childbirth, sexual health, sexual orientation, gender identity, birth control, abortion, pregnancy and childbirth, violence and abuse, and menopause. The WHC advocated institutional reform including pressuring hospitals, drug companies, and malpractice doctors and urged more women to enter the health labor force and encouraged those already in the labor force to agitate from within. The WHC also, Fishel added, played a crucial role in popularizing the ideas of the Women's Health Movement in first elaborating the ideology of Women's Liberation. Most interesting of all,

Fishel believed, was the focus in *Our Bodies, Our Selves* on the exchange of personal experience as well as research into professional sources.[102]

In April 1974, *Ramparts* published excerpts from Studs Terkel's *Working* (1974). His essay was titled "Women at Work." Terkel was perhaps America's most skilled practitioner of the art of simply letting people talk. A well-known radio broadcaster in Chicago, he had edited two remarkable books, *Division Street: America*, and *Hard Times: An Oral History of the Great Depression*, which were comprised of tape-recorded interviews with men and women in all classes across the American social landscape. Through the 1960s and into the 1970s, Terkel had traveled extensively around the country — his own Chicago, Brooklyn, mid-Western farms, the

---

[102] Elizabeth Fishel, "The Women's Self-Help Movement," *Ramparts Magazine*, November 1973, p. 30.

coal mining areas of Appalachia — recording what people had to say about their work.

From about one hundred of these interviews, *Ramparts'* editorial staff selected four case studies that delved into the lives and labor of American women pushed to the margins of society. They included: a portrait of Maggie Holmes, a downtrodden domestic laborer; Sharon Atkins, a receptionist; Grace Clements, a factory worker; and Lilith Reynolds, a poverty worker. Terkel's portraits sympathetically humanized these women and gave them an articulate voice that provided keen insight into the daily drudge and struggle of their lives. These four women lived in different parts of the nation and performed different jobs, but all of them shared one distinct thing in common: their labor was woefully exploited, which was exacerbated due to the fact that some were mothers raising children without the help of male breadwinners in a nation in which childcare was considered a privilege rather than a basic human right, which significantly derailed these and countless other women's aspirations for genuine social equality.

In June 1974, *Ramparts* published an article titled "The New Woman," contributed by Anaïs Nin, which was derived from a talk she had given in April 1973 in San Francisco as part of a celebration of women in the arts. Nin's "New Woman" was no historical reference to the bobbed hair flappers of the 1920s. Rather, she imagined the woman of the future, who she believed were being born in the early 1970s. This New Woman would, Nin explained, be a woman completely free of guilt for creating her self-development. She would be a woman in harmony with her own strength, not necessarily called masculine, or eccentric, or something unnatural. Man had, Nin noted, been uneasy about this self-evolution of woman, "but he need not be," she asserted, because, instead of having a dependent, he would have a true partner who would never try to live vicariously through him. "A woman can be courageous," Nin concluded, "can be adventurous, she can be all these things. And this new woman who is coming up is very inspiring, very wonderful."[103]

In September 1974, *Ramparts* published an article penned by Gene Marine, who was the author of *A Male Guide to Women's Liberation* (1972). His essay was titled "Sterilization: Who Decides?" In it he described the prominence of eugenics in 1970s America, noting several instances of forced sterilization of women who were welfare recipients. One such case study was about an African American woman named Nial Ruth Cox of North Carolina. The state of North Carolina had, Marine explained, ordered her

---

[103] Anais Nin, "The New Woman," *Ramparts Magazine*, June 1974, p. 44.

sterilization when she was seventeen years old. Her "problem" was simply that she was on welfare. Under the North Carolina statute that permitted the sterilization of Cox, there had been 1,107 sterilizations performed since 1964.

Brenda Feigen Fasteau was an attorney working with the Women's Rights Project of the American Civil Liberties Union. On behalf of Cox, Fasteau and the ACLU had brought suit against various North Carolina officials. The idea was to get North Carolina's law tossed out as unconstitutional on any of ten or a dozen different grounds. Of Cox, Fasteau said that she was not and never had been mentally defective, although the doctor who performed the operation asserted that she was. But no criterion whatsoever was used to determine this.

In the opinion of the ACLU, Cox was sterilized because she was black, a member of a welfare family and, at the time of the operation, a minor. The part about her being a minor was particularly egregious to Marine who noted that the national office of the ACLU had turned up cases of the forced sterilization of black welfare minors as young as eleven or twelve years old in Texas, Florida, Alabama and South Carolina. But the South, Marine stipulated, had no monopoly on either the racism or inhumanity at the root of forced sterilization. In 1974 there were, Marine explained, twenty-two states that permitted the forced sterilization of anyone whom a court found to be "mentally defective," and one of the twenty-two was California.

But perhaps nowhere, Maine added, was more committed to forced sterilization of welfare recipients than Aiken, South Carolina, which had a population of just more than 13,000. In the first half of 1973, among the welfare mothers who been to Aiken County Hospital, more than one third had been sterilized. Of those sterilized, seventeen of eighteen were black and ten of the eighteen were under the age of twenty five. Doctor Clovis Pierce, who had sterilized them, explained to a local newspaper: "I work hard to pay my taxes. I'm tired of having people come to me to have babies that will have to be supported by tax dollars." Marine concluded the article by noting Hitler's similar enthusiasm for the forced sterilization of what he, like Dr. Pierce, deemed to be "undesirables."[104]

Marine's essay was followed in the September 1974 edition of *Ramparts* by an article contributed by Melissa Sones titled "Giving Birth." The article provided readers with advice on how to best take control of the birth process, including not having the child in a hospital. However, if a woman did decide to give birth in a hospital, Sones urged her to know what to expect. Sones also compared and

---

[104] Gene Marine, "Sterilization: Who Decides?" *Ramparts Magazine*, September 1974, p. 15.

contrasted the options available to pregnant women in other parts of the world to the U.S. In places such as China, the Soviet Union, Sweden, Denmark and Czechoslovakia, trained professionals could, she explained, be summoned to a woman's home rather than her having to be trapped in a hospital during childbirth. In other words, her article made plain how progressive the childbirth experience was in other parts of the world compared to the U.S., and she offered potential alternatives for making childbirth less frightening and safer for American woman. Sones believed that one of the primary problems in the American healthcare system was that the doctor was, as she put it, the dictator of the process, rather than the experience being a genuine partnership between the woman giving birth and the medical professionals tasked with aiding the process.

Sones' essay was followed in the September 1974 edition of *Ramparts* by another article contributed by Fishel titled "Childbirth: A Feminist View." In it Fishel noted that the energy of the burgeoning Women's Health Movement, with its emphasis on options and a woman's right to control her own body, health activists and consumers around the country were in the early 1970s increasingly questioning the American way of childbirth. Not oblivious to the medical advances of the twentieth century, many women had nevertheless refused to accept what was too often a trade-off between safe, doctor-controlled childbirth and humane, mother-and family-centered maternity care.

Feminists had, Fishel explained, increasingly challenged standard hospital procedures and worked to change it for the benefit of the whole family unit, rather than for the convenience of the OB-GYN. In addition, feminists had sought viable alternatives to hospital births including home births, regional birth clinics, and maternity homes. Each of these alternatives, Fishel asserted, benefited the members of the "new family" in various ways, though none was entirely without risks. The availability of these options to all expectant mothers, rather than the advocacy of one method over another, was, Fishel argued, crucial to the program for change.

This choice—plus control over her environment and the procedure of her birth; maximum safety for herself and her newborn; and the integration of the birth experience into her own and her family's life—at least, said maternity care reformers, should be the expectant mother's basic human rights. Although the last half century had, Fishel explained, unarguably seen a significant improvement in infant survival, feminist critics argued that simultaneous exclusion of women healers, especially midwives, from the American childbirth establishment had alienated the mother from the person delivering her baby and had gradually, as she put it, dehumanized childbirth. And since ninety-seven percent of all OB-GYNs in the U.S. in 1974 were men, the once intensely woman-centered experience of childbirth became male-dominated and male-controlled during industrialization on both sides of the Atlantic.

Fishel thus especially championed the maternity home as an alternative to the strict choice between home versus hospital birth, which she believed could provide a creative solution to what she referred to as the childbirth dilemma. Combining both the friendly, warm atmosphere of the home with the safety and expertise of the hospital (plus maximum control by the mother of her birth experience), the maternity home could, she explained, be set up as a community health center offering information and services for every phase of the pregnancy, from prenatal care, nutritional and family counseling through delivery and extensive postpartum follow-up. Run by and for women, with midwives providing the bulk of the care, the birth center would also, Fishel added, charge on a low sliding-scale. And, she noted, in a country where, year after year, defense was the overwhelming federal budget priority, safe and fulfilling maternity care was, she lamented, relegated to the position of "weak sister." But, she concluded, "suppose the American woman were to feel proud throughout her pregnancy," and "capable and dignified during delivery, joyful postpartum, and confident in raising her child — just imagine what power she would have then."[105]

In October 1974, *Ramparts* published a review contributed by Sharon Curtin of Tillie Olsen's *Tell Me a Riddle* (1961)

---

[105] Elizabeth Fishel, "Childbirth: A Feminist View," *Ramparts Magazine*, September 1974, p. 40.

and *Yonnondio: From the Thirties* (1974), and Rebecca Harding Davis' *Life in the Iron Mills* (1972), Grace Paley's *The Little Disturbances of Man* (1959) and *Enormous Changes at the Last Minute* (1974). Perhaps the most common theme in Curtin's review was the difficulty of life as a woman in a capitalist bastion such as the U.S. Curtin was also very evidently a great admirer of these authors, who she believed to be trailblazers of women's liberation and literature.

Yonnondio: From the Thirties was written in the 1930s. It detailed the lives of the Holbrook family, depicting their struggle to survive during the 1920s. *Yonnondio* explored the life of the working-class family, as well as themes of motherhood, socioeconomic order, and the pre-Depression era in American history. *Life in the Iron Mills* was a short story written by Davis in 1861. The story was set in the factory world of the nineteenth century and was one of the earliest American realist works, and by the 1970s had emerged as an important text for those who studied labor and women's issues. It was also recognized as an innovative work, and introduced American readers to the bleak lives of industrial workers in the mills and factories of the nation as it industrialized.

Whether writing about relationships, sexy little girls, loving and bickering couples, angry suburbanites, frustrated jobseekers, or Jewish children performing in a Christmas play, Grace Paley captured the loneliness, poignancy, and humor of the human experience with great style in her collection of short stories, *Disturbances of Man*. Most of the stories reflected Paley's highly stylized conception of lower-class, immigrant, or second-generation "ethnic" New Yorkers. Plot and action were secondary; the author's primary concern seemed to be with the social milieu, and with the immediate thoughts and feelings of the people she portrayed. There were also several unwed mothers depicted in the collection of essays, most of them on welfare.

In November 1974, *Ramparts* published a pictorial essay titled "Meet Ms. Caucus: Cartoons." The essay included illustrations provided by Gary Trudeau and text provided by comedian Nora Ephron. The cartoons depicted the difficulty of parents and teachers trying to undo the centuries of gendered conditioning that had by 1974 become naturalized. Ephron hailed Trudeau's comic strip, which she hoped might be an "absolutely painless way" for parents to introduce their children to the tenants (economic, political, and psychological empowerment) of women's liberation.

Though there have been great strides since the 1970s made in terms of women achieving more equality in American society as directors, doctors, advertising agents, and many other occupations, there remained great hurdles for women to navigate in the twenty-first century. The vast majority of scientists and executives continued to be men, *Roe v. Wade* continued to be challenged by states (especially in the South), and women generally continued to earn less money than men for doing comparable work. And though the misogyny deeply embedded in American society was increasingly challenged in public forums, millions of housewives and women who described themselves as Pro Life Christians overwhelmingly supported serial misogynist Donald Trump, a man who weaponized sexism in the 2016 general election against Hillary Clinton. Trump also infamously admitted to sexually assaulting women in the widely publicized *Access Hollywood* soundbite that hit airwaves in the weeks before the 2016 general election. The fact that his admission did not disqualify him from the American Presidency speaks to how deeply entrenched and partisan feminism – the notion that women should be treated as equals of men – remained decades into the twenty-first century.

CHAPTER SIX

"America's Broken Healthcare System"

Editors and contributors to *Ramparts Magazine* championed the notion that access to good healthcare was a basic human right routinely denied to millions of Americans. There was perhaps no greater example of the dire gap that existed between the rich and poor in American society than in the realm of healthcare (or lack thereof depending on one's socioeconomic status). *Ramparts* depicted the healthcare industry as one of the most egregiously corrupt and broken aspects of the American social system in the 1960s and 1970s, which was but another glaring example of the corporate welfare that shaped American society in the 1960s and 1970s.

In November 1970, *Ramparts* published an essay titled "Kaiser: You Pay Your Money and You Take Your Chances," written by Judith Milgrom Carnoy, who was a staff member of Pacific Studies Center specializing in the health care field. Her article described an archaic multiphasic medical system at Kaiser's San Francisco hospital in which physicians were ostensibly "private entrepreneurs" that constituted an "army of pushcart vendors in an age of supermarkets."[106] Oddly, Carnoy noted, *Fortune, Scientific American, and CBSTV*, seemed to erroneously believe that Kaiser was a paragon of state-of-the art medical care.

Carnoy's article sought to undermine this notion. Nurses she interviewed had, for example, told her that mechanical failures at the hospital occurred with astonishing regularity, and the physicians themselves remained very unsure of the reliability of the test procedures associated with the multiphasic

---

[106] Judith Milgrom Carnoy, 'Kaiser: You Pay Your Money and You Take Your Chances," *Ramparts Magazine*, November 1970, p. 26.

screening computerized system, which often lost patients' records. Carnoy could not understand why, especially when considering that the multiphasic screening system was so unreliable, that Kaiser was expanding the program or why, considering how inefficient and alienating for its members the Kaiser Health Plan was, it was being hailed as an answer to "fix" the healthcare crisis in American society.

To answer these questions, Carnoy wrote, was to confront the malaise of market medicine and the incurability of its own chronic disorder. Centralized medical care under the market system, she explained, functioned against people because it was designed so that the system could never square private interest through private profit with the task of promoting the general welfare. There was as such, she lamented, a lot of talk about providing services (always shaped by market economics) for the community; but there was hardly a word about planning health services with the actual community it was meant to benefit.

The community recipient of health services, she argued, had a right to determine the structure and content of its health services, and that hospital workers around the country were at last beginning to organize around this issue, as well as around wages. But what the patients or the hospital workers knew was needed was, she lamented, unfortunately irrelevant because the government, the American Medical Association, the medical industry, and Kaiser were already deciding the kind of health care the community was going to get— whether the community actually liked it or not. And it would be, Carnoy explained, inefficient and insensitive; it would lose records and keep patients standing for hours against the wall; it would use the illusion that they were getting something cheap to keep them from complaining. But the real answer to

America's medical problems, she concluded, could not be found in solutions which did nothing more than offer sugar-coated versions of the same old priorities and medical incentive system. The fix for The United States' broken and for-profit healthcare system was not, she concluded, in Kaiser; it lied rather, in decentralized medical care, organized not for profit but for humanity.[107]

In February 1971, *Ramparts* published an essay aided by a grant from the Fund for Investigative Journalism titled "Madness in the Mental Health Industry," written by Andrew Kopkind and James Ridgeway, who were the editors of the Hard Times section of the magazine. Like Carnoy, they argued that the corporate nature of the healthcare industry was deleterious beyond the point of repair. Even the mental health profession was, the noted, fueled by a profit motive rather than by

---

[107] Ibid, p. 31.

the humanity of the patient. Corporate law much like the mental health profession, they wrote, defended helpless innocents while it solidified business and political monopolies. Corporate education provided useful instruction while it supported imperial extension. Corporate industry provided consumers their "plastic toys while it grabbed the nation's wealth." Corporate Mental Health too, the authors concluded, "soothed patients' nerves with drugs while keeping them mad."[108]

In July of 1971, *Ramparts* published an essay written by Frances Lang and James Ridgeway titled "Health Economics." In it they presented President Richard Nixon as King Midas because he often expressed a desire to make the American healthcare system better,

---

[108] Andrew Kopkind and James Ridgeway, "Madness in the Mental Health Industry," *Ramparts Magazine*, February 1971, p. 47.

but had actually sharply cut money spent for medical research and scholarships. Nixon's 1971 budget request, for example, involved cuts in hundreds of research projects, and for the second year in a row it made no provision for the construction of research facilities. To demonstrate his enthusiasm for training medical professionals, Nixon had, the essayists explained, asked for $12 million for student loans—a reduction of $3 million from the sum appropriated in 1970, and $14.5 million below that granted by Congress in 1969. Nixon signed the Emergency Health Personnel Act of 1970, which permitted health professionals to do alternative draft service by practicing medicine in areas where there were few doctors. But the act had, Lang and Ridgeway lamented, never been put into operation. Instead, the administration sought unsuccessfully to close down the Public Health Service clinics where many of the new doctors were to practice. Similarly, the President vetoed a bill to provide medical schools with money for development of family medical programs a few months after expressing in public his interest in such programs.

In September of 1971, *Ramparts* published another essay written by Ridgeway titled "The Economics of Health" in reaction to Senator Ted Kennedy's recent proposal to reform the American healthcare system. In it Ridgeway argued that although the Kennedy legislation seemed radical compared to Nixon's, close inspection suggested it might actually reinforce the existing structure. Under the Kennedy proposal, for example, amounts of money spent for healthcare would have been allocated by regions and based on prior health-spending patterns. That could mean, for instance, that the Northeast, which spent a lot on health, would continue to get a good deal of money for healthcare, while the South, which was much poorer and thus spent relatively little, would continue to get small amounts.

The creation of a health security board appointed by President Nixon was, Ridgeway explained, meant to change authority from the hospitals and doctors to the government, but, he added, the health industry already included government as an important part of its structure. The board, Ridgeway concluded, would thus likely perpetuate the inveterate deficiencies in the health industry by including representatives of government, Congressional committees, doctors, hospitals, drug companies and other suppliers, with consumers not included in policy-making decisions.

Ridgeway contributed yet another essay titled "Health; The Blue Cross We Bear," which was published in the April 1972 edition of *Ramparts*. In it he elaborated that the system being broken beyond repair was actually good business for Blue Cross-Blue Shield, whose contractors charged the federal government an administration fee for handling the federal health insurance program. That fee was set at 4.5 percent of costs. This fee, Ridgeway explained, provided a positive incentive to increase costs, thereby producing more income for administration. The contract was, he added, designed to increase expense and add inflation.[109]

In April of 1973, *Ramparts* published an expose titled "A Matter of Life and Death: The Scandalous Conditions at Boston City Hospital," written by Jonathan Kozol, who was a resident of Boston and the author of *Free Schools and Death at an Early Age* (1967). As the title of the essay suggests, there was widespread problems at Boston City Hospital, including not enough trained professionals such as anesthesiologists, which cost one of the women in Kozol's case studies her life. He argued that the endemic failures at Boston City

---

[109] James Ridgeway, "Health; The Blue Cross We Bear," *Ramparts Magazine*, April 1972, p. 26.

Hospital was but a microcosm of the endemic failures in the American healthcare system.

In February 1974, *Ramparts* published an essay titled "Hospitals for Sale (And Other Ways to Kill a Public Health System)," written Elinor Blake and Thomas Bodenheimer, both of whom were staff members of Health-PAC in San Francisco. Health-PAC was an organization that had researched the American health system since 1968. Blake and Bodenheimer described a kind of *Hunger Games*-like scenario that was the result of the "ominous trend in the nation's collapsing public health system," which included the closing of scores of county hospitals.

County hospitals, which were long maligned for their endless waiting lines, dirty and crowded wards, and rushed and impersonal treatment, were fast going the way of the Dodo. And twenty million "medically indigent" Americans, those who fell in the crack between Medicaid and health insurance, had, as a result of these closures, no place to go for basic medical care. These people—the seasonal farm workers, the black maid who earned $60 a week, the small owner whose business was failing, the warehouse loader out of work six months a year, the single alcoholic ineligible for welfare—were, Blake and Bodenheimer explained, dependent on public hospitals. The public hospitals that were not closed were systemically privatized.

And, the essayists added, as long as a small, underfinanced public system coexisted with a large, wealthy, private one, there would be competition for paying patients, doctors, money and power. And the private system would inevitably win. Thus the struggle to preserve the public system was, Blake and Bodenheimer asserted, more than the preservation of a rundown, half-empty, understaffed city or county hospital. It meant fighting to divert resources from private to public control. It meant attacking private hospitals when they took public money but left behind the public responsibility to care for everyone. "Eventually," Blake and Bodenheimer concluded, it meant "forcing the new, well-staffed local private hospital to become public."[110]

In July of 1974, *Ramparts* published an essay titled "National Health Insurance: The Care and Feeding of Medi-Business," written by Bodenheimer and Ronda Kotelchuck. They continued the pervasive theme of the American healthcare system being a de facto corporate welfare system designed to enrich the already wealthy at the expense of the indigent and sick.

Kotelchuck and Bodenheimer, however, seemed optimistic that in the midst of the Watergate crisis that National Health

---

[110] Elinor Blake and Thomas Bodenheimer, "Hospitals for Sale (And Other Ways to Kill a Public Health System)," *Ramparts Magazine*, February 1974, p. 33.

Insurance was soon to be a reality because Nixon was especially desperate for a popular social program to "save his skin" and there was likely to be a more liberal Congress in 1974. As such, they surmised that Blue Cross-Blue Shield would likely be more amenable to having a plan sanctioned by the conservative wings of the House and Senate than the alternative that might await if Democrats had the majority.[111]

Either way, the essayists noted, the National Health Insurance would prove to be a boon for what they referred to as the medical-industrial complex — the hospitals, insurance companies, nursing homes, medical supply and hospital construction industries, and all the other corporations that profited hand-over-fist from the sickness and death of poor Americans. The final NHI law that

---

[111] Ronda Kotelchuck and Thomas Bodenheimer, "National Health Insurance: The Care and Feeding of Medi-Business," *Ramparts Magazine*, July 1974, p. 27.

Bodenheimer and Kotelchuck prophesied would, they asserted, surely be a mixture of various bills, rather than the passage of just one coherent plan. And NHI would not, they predicted, arrive in one big leap; it was, they concluded, likely to come step by step over the next decade.

As sure as Kotelchuck and Bodenheimer were that NHI was inevitable, it was decades before the Affordable Care Act (Obamacare) was passed. The more equitable access to healthcare associated with the ACA was, however, vociferously attacked, challenged, and as undermined by corporate entities, lobbyists and politicians. The battle for socialized medicine did not, in short, abate. As such, the disparity in the quality of healthcare available to rich and poor Americans did not subside, a fact that was made glaringly apparent during the Covid-19 pandemic of 2020. The right for adequate medical care, in short, remained a dream deferred for tens of millions of Americans decades into the twenty-first century.

CHAPTER SEVEN

"The Rise of the Modern Environmentalism"

The New Left ardently championed the modern environmentalist movement, which clashed with the Old Left's disregard for the environment in favor of preserving the jobs of union workers. Modern environmentalism evolved out of an era in which mutually assured nuclear destruction seemed a likely possibility to destroy the planet and human civilization along with it. Rachel Carson's *Silent Spring* (1963) is considered one of the early works that gave voice to modern environmentalism. Carson's book helped awaken people to pesticides and destruction of the environment and along with it a litany of human ailments that although subtler and more gradual were every bit as destructive as was the specter of nuclear holocaust. *Ramparts Magazine,* the de facto voice of the American

New Left in the late-1960s and early 1970s, was, like Carson, at the forefront of the modern environmentalist movement, exposing readers to the fact that industrialization and economic development had grown all but synonymous with destruction of the natural world. The articles that comprise the body of this chapter are in chronological order to demonstrate how the modern environmental movement evolved and developed through the late-1960s and into the early 1970s, and to illuminate the very significant part that *Ramparts* played in demanding that humans had a right to live in a safe, healthy, and clean environment free from pollution and the specter of nuclear destruction.

The earliest essays *Ramparts* published pertaining to environmentalism focused mostly on the potential destruction of the planet with atomic and hydrogen bombs. But later essays focused more acutely on the exploitation of the environment in the interest of fueling an era of unfettered capitalism, of which often oil and plastic were common byproducts. In December 1966, *Ramparts* published an essay contributed by Barry Commoner, who was chairman of the Botany Department of Washington University, titled "Feasibility of Biological Recovery" based on a paper he had previously presented before a symposium on civil defense at the December 1965 meeting of the American Association for the Advancement of Science, in Berkeley, California. He provided a case study of what would become of the town of Cape May in the state of New Jersey in the event of a biological attack. He noted that Secretary of Defense Robert McNamara estimated that for a mere five billion dollars a system of shelters could save twenty-nine million Americans from nuclear attack. But the Cape May that folks returned to many years after the nuclear strike would not, Commoner noted, be worth returning to due to a complete lack of adequate heat, food, sanitation or medicine. Disease and starvation would also be rampant. In short, the feasibility for biological recovery was, as McNamara argued, promising. But Commoner helped to illuminate how dire that optimism was, and how completely insane the nuclear age, which promised ecological catastrophe, truly was.

"Feasibility of Biological Recovery" was followed immediately in the December 1966 edition of *Ramparts* by a second essay contributed by Commoner titled "Scenarios of Disaster: The Hudson Institute." He reviewed some of the scenarios on the consequences of nuclear war that had been developed by the Hudson Institute, one of the chief agencies that provided the government with analyses of civil defense problems. Commoner elaborated the catastrophic consequences of a nuclear attack on public health and was doubtful that the nation could recover from any of the Hudson Institute's scenarios. "We are in the process of constructing an unimaginably complex automatic war machine," he warned readers, "which encompasses the whole of our society and its natural environment."[112] Civil defense had, he further lamented, often been compared to an insurance policy. But an antimissile and shelter system were, he asserted, like a policy whose fine print restricted it to a very narrow range of circumstances. For this insurance policy Americans were, he explained, being asked to pay a staggering premium. "If we buy this policy," he wrote, "we are risking the very values which it is intended to preserve: the continued existence of this nation."[113] In other words, Commoner argued that the weapons Americans believed defended them were actually the biggest existential threat.

---

[112] Barry Commoner, "Scenarios of Disaster: The Hudson Institute," *Ramparts Magazine*, December 1966, p. 25

[113] Ibid, p. 25.

In April 1967, *Ramparts* published a two-part essay series written by Gene Marine titled "America the Raped." In part one of the series he turned his attention to the United States Army Corps of Engineers, which had proposed a network of canals, levees, dams, pumping stations and control centers designed to transform South Florida from largely underdeveloped swampland into black gold. This represented what Marine referred to as the engineers' "rape of America."[114] The key to the existence of South Florida — not its Miami Beach economic existence, but its ecological existence — was, Marine pointed out, the flow of water into Florida Bay, which mixed with the saltwater of the ocean to form one of the richest estuarine areas in the world. The Army Corp of Engineers' proposal promised to upset billions of years of ecological development in

---

[114] Gene Marine, "The Rape of America – Part I," *Ramparts Magazine*, April 1967, p. 35.

the name of real estate development and industrialization.

Part II of "America the Raped" further elaborated Marine's thesis that America was being subjected to an irreversible rapine by Engineers — "the people whose only approach to any question was to build something, manage something, or change something."[115] The principal failure of the engineers' mentality was, Marine argued, that they did not understand the concept of ecology; and one principal failure in dealing with them was that most other people did not understand ecology very much either. He thus concluded the essay by educating readers on the dire impact of ecological development as a result of the creation of gated communities and strip malls built without considering the effect on the system in which it was built, such as suburban South Florida's dire impact on the Everglades,

---

[115] Gene Marine, "The Rape of America – Part II," *Ramparts Magazine*, April 1967, p. 40.

which had dire implications for the state's swamps and estuaries, not to mention the diverse ecosystem home to millions different kinds of lifeforms. The genetic information contained in species populations, as well as the ecological information content of the total functioning array of organisms in an ecological system, represented an irreplaceable resource, Marine warned. "The freedom of the growth-rate planner, the builder of projects, the rapacious Engineer" foreshadowed, he concluded, "the death of man."[116]

In September 1969, *Ramparts* published an essay titled "Eco-Catastrophe!" written by Dr. Paul Ehrlich, who was a prominent ecologist, a professor of biology at Stanford University, and the co-author of *The Population Bomb* (1968), which portentously warned of the mass starvation of humans in the 1970s and 1980s due to overpopulation, as well as other

---

[116] Ibid, p. 49.

major societal upheavals. Ehrlich thus his essay concluded by advocating immediate action to limit population growth. Fears of a "population explosion," he wrote, were widespread in the 1950s and 1960s, but the book and its author brought the idea to an even wider and more receptive audience thanks to *Ramparts*. "Eco-Catastrophe!" recycled many of the alarmist ideas and warnings Ehrlich first proffered in *The Population Bomb*.

Barry Commoner, however, argued that Ehrlich focused too much on overpopulation as the source of environmental problems, and that their proposed solutions were politically unacceptable because of the coercion that they implied, and because the cost would fall disproportionately on the poor. He argued that technological and social development would inevitably lead to a natural decrease in both population growth and environmental damage.[117] And though some of the predictions were overly alarmist and inaccurate, the author alerted readers to the importance of environmental issues, such as global warming, which was almost totally ignored by the mainstream American media during the rise of the Affluent Society. And like Carson's *Silent Spring*, *The Population Bomb* and "Eco-Catastrophe!" were designed, above all, to coerce a conversation on the horrendous ecological costs of the Affluent Society.

In January 1970, *Ramparts* published an essay titled "Alaska---The Ecology of Oil" written by Barry Weisberg, who was a free-lance writer and co-director of the Bay Area Institute. The article described the destruction

---

117 Barry Commoner (May 1972). "A Bulletin Dialogue: on "The Closing Circle – A Response." *Bulletin of the Atomic Scientists*: 17–56. Population control (as distinct from voluntary, self-initiated control of fertility), no matter how disguised, involves some measure of political repression, and would burden the poor nations with the social cost of a situation—overpopulation—which is the current outcome of their previous exploitation, as colonies, by the wealthy nations.

of Alaska in the interest of oil exploration and mineral exploitation. Weisberg bemused the destruction of the earth – the source of all life – to accumulate wealth for shareholders of stock in multinational corporations. Humans, he warned, "were losing control." They were, he elaborated, "destroying the air we breathe, the water we drink, and the land we walk upon." And this was not an accident, he explained. It was rooted in the fundamental attitudes and practices of advanced industrial societies around the world. It was, he asserted, part of the "logic of capitalism," but it was also very much the result of the relationship humans had long assumed toward the natural world.[118] The talk about shifting from an economy of affluence, obsolescence, redundancy and waste to an economy that recognized scarcity must yield, he argued, demanded "practical

---

[118] Barry Weisberg, "Alaska---The Ecology of Oil," *Ramparts Magazine*, January 1970, p. 33.

proposals for a new economics." And those proposals had to include the mandatory recycling of all-natural resources; the mandatory production of only recyclable containers; the rationing of all-natural resources— especially rationing to provide for sane limits on the amount of consumption as well as to equalize mechanisms for distribution. Industrial processes must, he asserted, also be rationed as to the amount of oxygen, water or minerals they could consume in production. These were, he admitted, no small matters, but they were only the basic parameters for what would be the beginning of what he described as "a truly democratic policy for human's life support systems." It was thus imperative, he argued, that what he referred to as the "economy of death" needed to be replaced by an "economy of life." In Alaska, which was still mostly a distant frontier in the early 1970s, he saw an opportunity to stem the tide of exploitative industrial development of resources by creating a comprehensive democratically determined land use policy, in order to devise environmental regulatory agencies with adequate means of enforcement, to develop new forms of revenue sharing and community control over economic growth, and for humans to re-learn their agrarian inclinations toward nature. "While this must happen in Alaska," he wrote, "it must also happen on a national and global level" because the powers that shaped the fate of Alaska were also rooted in places far distant it, such as New York City and Washington D.C., "We must slow down," he concluded. "We must come to enjoy the world gently, remembering that this fragile earth is more to be admired than used, more to be cherished than exploited."[119]

In May 1970, just weeks after the first Earth Day was celebrated around the world,

---

[119] Barry Weisberg, "Alaska---The Ecology of Oil," *Ramparts Magazine*, January 1970, p. 33.

the editors of *Ramparts* dedicated its entire edition to championing environmentalism. The first essay published in the May 1970 edition of *Ramparts* was titled "Toward an Ecological Solution," contributed by Murray Bookchin. He argued that the "pollution problem" in 1970 was much worse than most a generation earlier could have imagined. The public as such increasingly sought personal and legislative solutions to pollution problems. Its supreme pontiff was, Bookchin wrote, consumer advocate Ralph Nader. The new pollutants were, Bookchin explained, no longer "poisons" in the popular sense of the term; rather they belonged to the problems of ecology, not merely pharmacology, and these unfortunately did not lend themselves to legislative redress.[120] The complexity and diversity of life that marked biological evolution over many millions of years was also

---

[120] Murray Bookchin, "Toward an Ecological Solution," *Ramparts Magazine*, May 1970, p. 7.

fast being replaced by a simpler, more synthetic and increasingly homogenized environment. Aside from any aesthetic considerations, the elimination of this complexity and diversity may, Bookchin explained, prove to be the "most serious loss of all." Modern society was, he continued, literally undoing the work of organic evolution. If this process continued unabated, he warned, the earth may be reduced to a level of biotic simplicity where humanity — whose welfare depended profoundly upon the complex food chains in the soil, on the land surface and in the oceans — would no longer be able to sustain itself as a viable animal species.[121]

Bookchin's essay was followed in the May 1970 edition of *Ramparts* by an article titled "Catch 24,400" contributed by Roger Rapoport, who was a co-author of *Is the Library Burning?* (1969) in which he chronicled two

---

[121] Ibid, p. 10.

massive fires, one in 1957 and the other in 1969, at the Rocky Flats Nuclear Production Facility in Colorado, fifteen miles outside of Denver. Both fires led to radioactive contamination both inside and outside of the facility. The 1969 fire was so severe that it led local health officials to perform independent tests of the area surrounding Rocky Flats to determine the extent of the contamination. This resulted in the first releases of information to the public that populated areas southeast of Rocky Flats had been contaminated. Releases from previous years had not been reported publicly prior to the fire; airborne-become-groundborne radioactive contamination extending well beyond the Rocky Flats plant was not publicly reported until the 1970s. Rapoport, in fact, seemed more appalled by the massive coverup of the disaster than the disaster itself. The 1969 fire and subsequent reports about it, including Rapoport's, helped to raise public awareness of potential hazards posed by the Rocky Flats plant and dozens of others and led to years of increasing citizen protests and demands for action and reform. Weapons production at Rocky Flats was finally halted after a combined FBI and EPA raid in 1989. The plant has since been shut down, with its buildings demolished and completely removed from the location, which is now a superfund site.

"Catch 24,400" was followed in the May 1970 edition of *Ramparts* by an essay titled "The Making of a Pollution-Industrial Complex," contributed by Martin Gellen, who was an associate of the Bay Area Institute for Policy Studies. The article, which included a cartoon drawing of a gleeful oilman in a pinstripe suit gladly shaking hands with a Park Ranger wearing Department of the Interior insignia, perpetuated the theme of corporate welfare that was particularly common in *Ramparts*. Gellen argued that the chemical industry provided the most glaring example of what her referred to as, "the incest between the pollution control business and the industrial polluters."[122] The chemical industry was, Gellen asserted, in the enviable position of reaping sizable profits by attempting to clean up rivers and lakes (at public expense), which they had profitably polluted in the first place. To facilitate this, Gellen added, practically every major chemical company in the U.S. had established a pollution abatement division or was in the process of doing so. Dow Chemical, for example, produced a wide variety of products and services for water pollution abatement, including measuring instruments, specialty treatment chemicals, and a special biological filter medium called SURF-PAC. The company designed, engineered, built and serviced wastewater treatment plants and was also supervising municipal sewage plants in Cleveland and working on waste disposal problems for lumber companies in Pensacola,

---

[122] Martin Gellen, "The Making of a Pollution-Industrial Complex," *Ramparts Magazine*, May 1970, p. 23.

Florida, and West Nyack, New York. All of these projects were funded by American taxpayer via the Federal Water Pollution Control Administration (FWPCA). In other words, the proverbial wolves were tasked with cleaning up the metaphorical chicken coup, which was actually paid for by the average American, for the benefit of the corporations who profited from polluting the environment in the first place. It was, Gellen believed, corporate welfare at its worst. The crisis of the environment, Gellen explained, needed to be viewed in terms of a paradox central to modern society. The mobilization of the productive energies of society and the physical forces of nature for the purpose of accumulating profits or enhancing private power and privilege conflicted directly with the universal dependence of men upon nature for the means of their common survival. As such, he argued, a society whose principal ends and incentives were monetary and expansionist inevitably produced material and cultural impoverishment — in part precisely because of the abundance of profitable goods. To make an industry out of cleaning up the mess that industry itself made was a logical extension of corporate capitalism. What was needed, he concluded, was not an extension of what was already bad, but its transformation into something much better.[123]

Gellen's "The Making of a Pollution-Industrial Complex" was followed by as essay titled "Para-Real Estate: The Handing Out of Resources" contributed by James Ridgeway, who was the author of *Closed Corporation: American Universities in Crisis* (1969). The theme of the wolves cleaning up the chicken coup continued in Ridgeway's article. Traditionally, Ridgeway explained, the ally of and lobbyist for the "oil and gas gang," the Department of the Interior, had always been the mediator

---

[123] Ibid, p. 28.

between the industrialists and the White House. Although it was officially self-styled as a "conservationist" agency, the Department was actually, Ridgeway asserted, much busier in its role as a brokerage handing out contracts to competing interests. Overseeing five-hundred million acres of public land, as well as more than a million square miles of territory on the outer continental shelf, the Department of the Interior was in fact "the biggest real estate agency in the world."[124] The way it played the real estate game, Ridgeway explained, showed what presidents actually meant when they referred to conservation. For Richard Nixon and Lyndon Johnson before him, Ridgeway elaborated, "conservation functioned as the facade behind which environmental pollution was formalized and made part of a society that had come to depend on environmental pollution to fuel its

---

[124] James Ridgeway, "Para-Real Estate: The Handing Out of Resources," *Ramparts Magazine*, May 1970, p. 33.

GDP." Interior thus, Ridgeway wrote, served as a commissioned broker, opening the outer continental shelf for oil exploration and soothing the citizens of places such as Santa Barbara, California, when there was an oil spill by telling them all about new safety regulations, modern valves for oil rigs, and so on, while the drilling and spills continued unabated. Environmental pollution was, Ridgeway asserted, unavoidable in a society where business depended lock-stock-and barrel on a steadily increasing demand for consumer goods. Conservation, according to the government's concept of the idea, thus became a program for organizing the white, suburban middle class, much in the same way as "consumer protection" had organized them in the 1960s. Like "consumer protection," the "new conservation" was "unraveling into a fake ideology," consciously developed for and by supposedly liberal-minded people who had made a pretty good life for themselves by, among other things, exploiting the land and water.[125] In other words, capitalists expressing fret about the environment was, Ridgeway believed, patently Orwellian considering capitalism was the primary source of environmental degradation. Unless capitalism was checked and reformed completely, the destruction of the world's ecosystem was but a tragically inevitable consequence of industrial development.

Marine's essay was followed in the May 1970 edition of *Ramparts* by an article titled, "Why the Population Bomb Is a Rockefeller Baby," contributed by Steve Weissman, who was a member of the Pacific Studies Center in Palo Alto, California, which was a research collective specializing in the social, political and economic dimensions of American capitalism. The group's projects ranged from studies and publications on U.S. involvement

---

[125] Ibid, p. 33.

in the Third World, multinational corporations, labor problems, high finance and environmental destruction, to films on ecology and inflation. Marine argued that John D. Rockefeller III was largely responsible for the dire predictions of the "population bomb" proffered by Ehrlich (see above). In 1952 the chairman of the Rockefeller Foundation, hosted a highly select conference on population in Colonial Williamsburg, Virginia. To this showpiece of historical conservation came some thirty of the nation's most eminent conservationists, public health experts, Planned Parenthood leaders, agriculturalists, demographers and social scientists. After two and a half days of intensive discussion, they agreed to form a new group that could act as "a coordinating and catalytic agent in the broad field of population."[126] The Rockefeller led group was dedicated to confronting the

---

[126] Steve Weissman, "Why the Population Bomb Is a Rockefeller Baby," *Ramparts Magazine*, May 1970, p. 42.

perils of overpopulation by championing the family planning movement. Family planning services were defined as educational, comprehensive medical or social activities that enabled individuals, including minors, to determine freely the number and spacing of their children and to select the means by which this might be achieved. Family planning also involved consideration of the number of children a woman wished to have, including the choice to have no children at all, as well as the age at which she wished to have them.

These matters were influenced by external factors such as marital situation, career considerations, financial position, and any disabilities that might affect their ability to have children and raise them. If sexually active, family planning might also involve the use of contraception and other techniques to control the timing of reproduction. Other techniques commonly used included sexuality education, prevention and management of sexually transmitted infections, pre-conception counseling and management, and infertility management. Family planning as defined by the United Nations and the World Health Organization encompassed services leading up to conception and thus did not promote abortion as a family planning method, although levels of contraceptive use reduced the need for abortion. Weissman feared that such top-down central planning and social engineering signaled a new phase of imperialism and could be used to justify social Darwinian genocide and imperial control, as well as oppression of minorities and disadvantaged groups or even a re-popularization of eugenics. It should, he argued, be up to each nation to determine how best to balance resources and population and not the purview of American extra-governmental organizations such as the Population Council. Where there was greater economic security, political participation, elimination of gross class division, liberation of women, and respected leadership, humane and successful population programs were most promising, Weissman explained. Without these conditions, he concluded, genocide was "nicely masked by the welfare imperialism of the West."[127] In other words, just as capitalism was at the root of pollution, it was also at the root of the population bomb that seemed so apocalyptic to so many in the early decades of the 1970s.

"Why the Population Bomb Is a Rockefeller Baby" was followed by an essay titled "The Eco-Establishment" contributed by Weissman and Katherine Barkley, who was a staff member at the Pacific Studies Center. They noted that environmentalism was not wholesale supported by other leftist movements because. For instance, if one were to ask young African American activists about

---

[127] Ibid, p. 47.

the movement to save the ecosystem, many of them, Weissman and Barkley explained, would tell you that it was a way of distracting attention from the old movement that was supposed to save their skins. Barkley and Weissman, however, noted that all segments of the New Left needed to unite behind the overriding goal of "unfouling America's common nest" before was too late by "turning back the pages of the environmental doomsday clock." Once the environmental movement had succeeded, they asserted, the revolutionaries could then get back to the questions that defined the social movements of the 1960s.[128] But environmentalism would, they declared, "be the primary issue of the 1970s" because such stewards of the nation's wealth as the Ford Foundation, with its Resources for the Future, Inc. (RFF), and Laurence Rockefeller's Conservation Foundation needed a grass-roots

---

[128] Katherine Barkley and Steve Weissman, "The Eco-Establishment," *Ramparts Magazine*, May 1970, p. 49.

movement to help consolidate their control over national policymaking, bolster their hold over world resources, and escalate further cycles of useless economic growth.[129] Echoing Weissman's article that preceded it, the essayists further argued that the American auto industry was combating waste only so it could afford to pollute even more; it was, Weissman and Barkley lamented, planning to produce more (smog-controlled) private autos to crowd more highways, which meant even more advertising to create more "needs" to be met by planned obsolescence. Socially, Weissman and Barkley warned, the result would prove disastrous. Ecologically, "it could be the end." In other words, rather than abolishing capitalism, which was at the root of the rapid environmental degradation associated with the Affluent American Society of the 1950 and 1960s, capitalists, including America's otherwise "liberal" politicians,"

---

[129] Ibid, p. 49.

were engaged in a "rhetoric of reform" that actually sought to treat an infected wound by infecting it even more.

The final essay specifically pertaining to the environmentalism movement published in the May 1970 edition of *Ramparts* was titled "Science and the Gross National Pollution" contributed by George M. Woodwell, who was a senior ecologist at Brookhaven National Laboratory and a lecturer at Yale University. He noted the numerous fishes, such as mackerel in California and Coho of Lake Michigan, which due to pollution were in danger of extinction. He prophesied that many kinds of fish would disappear in the coming decades. Woodwell believed that the continued failure of American science to address itself to such problems clearly and effectively was the most disturbing aspect of the catastrophic destruction of the global ecosystem. "How can it be," Woodwell rhetorically asked readers, "that the American scientific establishment, whose ingenuity and technology appear often to be almost infinitely versatile, is fumbling with the crisis of the environment?" Science should, he asserted, have been intensely concerned with the devastation of the earth long before conspicuous disasters and grass-roots protests made ecology fashionable.

But scientists had not, he lamented, been leaders in the protest, and by 1970 they were, to his great dismay, conspicuously unprepared for the environmental crisis and some were even often antagonistic towards reform.[130] He chronicled how the science community had in the decades after World War II been so thoroughly co-opted by multinational corporations such as Dow Chemical that science was a primary reason for the ecological catastrophe that so many leftists in the early 1970s felt compelled to confront.

---

[130] George M. Woodwell, "Science and the Gross National Pollution," *Ramparts Magazine*, May 1970, p. 51.

Woodwell was also not optimistic about a sea change anytime soon, especially considering that the scientific community was, as he noted, more aligned with corporations seeking to enrich shareholders as quickly and efficiently as possible, instead of finding a balance between humanitarianism and scientific research. In other worlds, science had been married to the interests of capitalism rather than to social responsibility and sustainability, which had dire consequences for all of humanity.

In March 1971, *Ramparts* published an essay titled "The Cleaning of America: Don't Hold Your Breath," contributed by Ridgeway. He expressed incredible pessimism that America would ever be able to adequately address the dire pollution crisis that existed in the United States because the most powerful entities in the nation, who, he noted, also held a great deal of political power, benefited hand over fist from pollution. The large utilities and the big oil companies, he explained, also worked in tandem. The utilities corporations "propagandized the constant energy crisis," demanding the right to build more electric plants, which consumed more oil, gas, coal and uranium. At the same time the utilities corporations publicly bemoaned the energy crisis, they were actually selling electricity, encouraging homeowners to leave the lights on outside all night long to scare away burglars, or establishing tie-in sales with home developers in an effort to persuade them to build all-electric homes.

This coalition may well become more open and defined, Ridgeway predicted, because the big oil companies owned vast tracts of land in the United States, which they eventually would begin to develop into new towns that sapped more energy, which would inevitably cause even more pollution. The Nixon administration, he noted, advocated the concept of "new towns" because they represented new markets to exploit. New towns—built on oil company land by electric utility conglomerates and financed by oil companies—would, Ridgeway prophesied, be marketed as the most modern and clever solutions to the problems of population congestion and ecological decay. But in truth, he concluded, the new town concept merely "closed the circle of the energy monopoly" and thus ensured more ecological destruction.[131]

The prominent theme of corporations exploiting peoples, places, and things in order to maximize shareholders' wealth was especially the tenor of an article *Ramparts* published in October 1971 tiled "Rocky Mountain Coal Fever," written by Ridgeway that depicted oil and coal companies working in tandem to destroy Colorado's ecology. He was most concerned by the variety of toxic

---

[131] James Ridgeway, "The Cleaning of America: Don't Hold Your Breath," *Ramparts Magazine*, March 1971, p. 18.

chemical compounds, especially those composed of mercury, moving through the biosphere of Colorado. In addition to heightened chances for cancer as a result of these toxins, many of the compounds in the biosphere also heightened the risk for birth defects and could diminish oxygen levels in the atmosphere. The fact that all this was done to enrich the coffers of corporate shareholders to the detriment of everyone else seemed to Ridgeway to be criminally amoral.

In November 1971, *Ramparts* published an essay titled "Disney's War Against the Wilderness" written by Roger Rapoport, who had recently published a book titled *The Great American Bomb Machine* (1971). His essay included a cartoon of a sinister rodent similar in features to Mickey Mouse standing firmly in front of a sign with the word "Mineral" followed by "Kingdom." "Mineral" had been crossed out and replaced by "Magic." Rapoport chronicled Disney's attempts to build an Alpine ski resort in Mineral King Valley, California. Disney's plan sparked a heated battle between the developers of the proposed resort and the Sierra Club. The battle centered on the fact that six miles of a proposed all-weather access road would cut through Sequoia National Park, displacing some eight million cubic yards of rock and dirt. As Disney launched a three-year snow study and finalized its plans, the Sierra Club dutifully lobbied the National Park Service to block the construction of the highway. But after the Park Service and its supervisor, interior secretary Stewart Udall, approved the road, the Sierra Club resorted to litigation. On June 5, 1969, it sued the heads of Sequoia National Park and Sequoia National Forest and the interior and agriculture secretaries in federal court, arguing that the project improperly handed control of too much national forest land to Disney and that the highway through the national park was illegal. A trial judge then issued a preliminary injunction, halting work until the case reached the Supreme Court.

The high court struck the Sierra Club a blow on April 19, 1972, when it ruled against the organization on procedural grounds in *Sierra Club v. Morton*. In a 4-3 decision, the court held that the organization—founded by John Muir in 1892—lacked standing to sue because it had not shown how exactly the proposed ski resort would injure any individuals, as opposed to the collective interests of the Sierra Club's membership. But even as the Supreme Court handed Disney and the Forest Service a victory, another legal obstacle stalled construction of the highway. On January 1, 1970, President Nixon signed the National Environmental Policy Act, which required federal agencies to study the environmental effects of proposed actions in detail before building. The Sierra Club subsequently amended its lawsuit to conform to the Supreme Court's standing doctrine, and the Forest Service prepared several drafts of its environmental impact statement. It released the final 285-page tome (nearly 600 pages, including appendices) in February 1976. By then, Disney's proposal was more than a decade old, and the company's executive leadership—along with skiing enthusiasts and many members of the government—had lost interest in Mineral King. Congress finally killed the project with the National Parks and Recreation Act of 1978. With President Jimmy Carter's signature on November 10, 1978, the Mineral King area became part of Sequoia National Park. Rapoport's explication of the Mineral Valley conflict summed up, he believed, the damage done to Disney's longstanding image of environmental friendliness. The beautiful old Disney nature films produced by the company in the 1950s were, he explained, only an "illusion;" the reality was "the determination to use all the corporation's considerable goodwill and political clout to take over via the U.S. Forest Service at Mineral King." It was, Rapoport concluded, "the end to all our childhood fantasies: Mickey Mouse and Smokey the Bear conspiring to tear up the wilderness."[132]

Today, Mineral King Valley is still accessible only by the old mining-era wagon path — now a one-lane automobile road — but most of the land is now a federally designated wilderness. For the Sierra Club, the Mineral King controversy marked a significant turning point in the organization's history. The Club was founded in 1892 with a two stated purpose: "exploring, enjoying, and rendering accessible the mountain regions of the Pacific Coast" and "preserving the forests and other features of the Sierra Nevada Mountains." Over time, the growth of automobile tourism in national parks and battles over dams in

---

[132] Roger Rapoport, "Disney's War Against the Wilderness," *Ramparts Magazine*, November 1971, p. 33.

Yosemite's Hetch Hetchy Valley and Colorado's Echo Park showed that those two purposes were not necessarily compatible. The Sierra Club's priorities thus shifted accordingly. When the Forest Service first proposed a ski resort in Mineral King in 1949, the Club pledged its support. In 1965, the Club's national board of directors had reversed its stance—but only by a split vote of seven to four. By the end of the Mineral King conflict in 1978, however, the club had firmly established its New Left environmentalist credentials.

In February 1972, *Ramparts* published an essay titled "Clean Water: Nixon Vetoes Nixon," written by Ridgeway. Nixon's environmental policies achieved what Ridgeway described as "a new level of farce" when the administration turned against the water pollution legislation it originally had urged Congress to adopt.[133] William

---

[133] James Ridgeway, "Clean Water: Nixon Vetoes Nixon," *Ramparts Magazine*, February 1972, p. 6.

Ruckelshaus, administrator of the Environmental Protection Agency, Ridgeway noted, helped both to write the bill and push it through the Senate, only to discover that the White House was opposing it. Ridgeway surmised that Nixon had grown leery of being perceived by corporations as something other than a great friend to industrial development, which water pollution legislation would have surely impeded by imposing more stringent standards on the amounts of waste and refuse that corporations could legally pump and dump into America's intrastate waterways.

In March 1972, *Ramparts* published another essay contributed by Rapoport titled "Oops!...The Story of Nuclear Power Plants," part of which chronicled the actions of a whistleblower named Robert Rowen, Jr., who began working as a nuclear control technician at PG&E's Humboldt Bay Power Plant in 1964. Rowen had reported his former employer for what he perceived to be major safety violations relating to radiation exposure of colleagues. At a May 20, 1970, company safety meeting, Rowen and his then colleague Forest Williams testified to the information they had gathered to representatives of the Atomic Energy Commission, which was the federal agency that used to oversee and regulate uses of atomic and nuclear energy in the U.S. Both men were ultimately fired from the company within weeks of their testimony. After being fired from PG&E, Rowen brought his findings to the Atomic Energy Commission, which found that PG&E had not committed any major safety violations relating to radiation exposure in its investigation. It was, Rapoport indicated, another case of industry insider being tasked with regulating a broken and corrupt industry that inevitably led to destruction of the natural environment and human life. Six years after Rowen was fired, the nuclear power plant section of the Humboldt Bay Power Plant, known as Unit 3, was finally shut down due to required seismic upgrade costs.

In August 1973, *Ramparts* published a report titled, "Land Reform: Reclaiming Mother Earth," contributed by Warren Weber, who had been involved in setting up a community land trust in California. In the article, Weber described the first National Land Reform Conference that he had recently attended in San Francisco. The attendees of the conference represented movements comprising environmentalists, cooperatives, consumers, family farmers, mineworkers, farm workers, urban and rural poor, Indian, Chicano, and black and white populations. What united this diverse cadre of conferees was, Weber explained, a deep concern about concentrated corporate power over land, the emphasis being on "concentrated," not necessarily "corporate." He noted that two percent of the households in the U.S. owned eighty percent of all individually held corporate stock and ninety percent of all individually held corporate bonds. Weber was, however, optimistic that establishing land trusts could gradually offset this inequity. The more land that was held in land trusts was more land that could be sustainably cultivated concomitant to being preserved from corporate exploitation and environmental degradation.

In December 1973, *Ramparts* published another essay contributed by Gene Marine titled, "Scorecard on the Environment." In it, he lamented the dire need for recycling programs and begrudged the fact that the government had failed to make recycling the law and had failed to build recycling plants. He further explained that the energy crisis would soon bring Americans to their knees, which rather than bolstering environmentalism would actually undermine it. "The same citizen who was all excited about Earth Day 1970," he bemoaned, was "going to follow the industrialists in blaming it on us 'ecological extremists.'" He, however, concluded by declaring that the most feasible way of stemming the tide of the destruction of the planet and all humankind along with it was a full-fledged revolution against the capitalist system, which inevitably destroyed the global ecosystem in the name of economic "development."

In March 1973, *Ramparts* published an editorial contributed by Derek Shearer in which he hailed the environmental movement that had gained traction and influence since the first Earth Day celebration in April 1970. In the 1972-midterm elections, environmental propositions were, he noted, passed by voters in Colorado (the Winter Olympics issue) and California (the initiative to preserve the coastline), and a number of politicians were elected to Congress on ecology-oriented platforms. Court actions against factories and power plants that polluted the environment also continued to meet with success. Still, he regretted, the ecology movement-such as it was—lacked a sophisticated understanding of the relationship between the environment and the politico-economic system. He thus provided a bibliography of newly published books that could help readers better understand the complex symbiosis between the environment and the politico-economic system. Some of the texts included many written by writers and editors affiliated with or on staff at *Ramparts*, such as: Barry Commoner's *The Closing Circle-Nature, Man & Technology*; James Ridgeway's *The Politics of Ecology* and *The Last Play*; and Barry Weisberg's *Beyond Repair: The Ecology of Capitalism*; and Matt Edel's *Economics and Ecology*.

In August 1973, *Ramparts* published an essay titled "Powers That Be: The *NBC* Documentary You Never Got to See," contributed by Elliot Kanter, who chronicled the work of an award-winning and acclaimed documentary filmmaker named Don Widener, who took his Los Angeles crew as far afield as the Baltic Sea to gather evidence for his documentary series about the destruction of the world ecological system. "Timetable for Disaster" was a consideration of global water pollution problems. "A Sea of Troubles" uncovered the unhappy lot of fishermen and fisheries on both the Atlantic and Pacific coasts of the U.S. due to mercury and DDT infesting fish. "Powers that Be" was a harsh and frightening look at the activities of the Atomic Energy Commission. The film was ultimately broadcast despite pressure from the AEC to keep it off the air and the agency's attempts to impede production along the way. Although these shows were described by Kanter as being of the highest quality and part of a series which any other local station in the nation would be hard-pressed to match, they, Kanter lamented, seemed to be at an end: Widener's contract was, Kanter explained, not picked up by the network he worked for. Kanter insinuated that Widener's contract was not renewed because he was an environmentalist who shined a glaring spotlight on corporations that were conglomerated with *NBC*, his former employer. The title of Kanter's essay, "The Powers That Be," was thus a pun that referred to one of Widener's documentaries, but also the powers that decided not to renew his contract or air his muckraking documentary series which was dedicated to exposing viewers to environmentalist discourse.

In August 1974, *Ramparts* published another essay written by Gene Marine titled "Moratorium: Taking the Initiative in California." In it, he urged Californians to demand safer and cleaner alternative sources of renewable energy to power the state's businesses and homes. He argued that if California voters really believed that they faced an energy shortage, then their answer was not to switch to another fossil fuel and to continue to depend on one central and monopolistic source such as Pacific Gas & Electric. Their answer was, Marine asserted, to force industrial power users to push for the development of alternatives (such as solar and wind power) that could be "decentralized" thereby putting power in the hands of average Californians rather than corporate giants.[134]

Marine's essay was followed in the August 1974 edition or *Ramparts* by an article titled "Nuclear Power: Lying Doesn't Make It Safe," contributed by Tom Zeman, who chronicled Veteran California Congressman Chester "Chet" Holifield, who was best known as the chief Congressional guardian of the nuclear power program. Holifield had convinced President Nixon in 1971 that the as-yet impractical "breeder reactor" — a nuclear power reactor that produced more plutonium than it used — was the answer to America's future energy needs. He assured Nixon that the

---

[134] Gene Marine, "Moratorium: Taking the Initiative in California," *Ramparts Magazine*, August 1974, p. 32.

president could provide the U.S. with an inexhaustible source of energy for $3 billion ($47 billion less than it cost to put a man on the moon). By June of 1971, Nixon was calling the breeder reactor America's best hope for meeting the nation's growing demand for economical clean energy. But despite the president's enthusiasm, and the generous Congressional funding (thanks, again, largely to Holifield), the breeder program, and the whole U.S. nuclear power program, seemed in 1974 to be in deep trouble. The first commercial breeder reactor nearly exploded when it started up in 1966, and was finally shut down for good after continued troubles and inefficiency. A demonstration breeder, about one third the size of those envisioned for commercial use, would not be completed until 1983, at a cost of a billion dollars.

Though rhetorically a champion of small government, the Nixon administration was actually quite expansionist, as evidenced by the creation of the Energy Research and Development Administration, which was championed by Holifield as an entity that could help make his dream of an America fueled by "breeder reactors" a reality. The agency was created as part of the Energy Reorganization Act of 1974, which was passed in the wake of the 1973 OPEC oil crisis. The act split the Atomic Energy Commission into two new agencies: the Nuclear Regulatory Commission, which would regulate the commercial nuclear power industry, while the ERDA, which would manage the energy research and development, nuclear weapons, the naval reactors program and breeder reactors. In other words, even when the federal government seemed to commit to finding alternative sources of energy, they were centralized systems and industrialized operations that could potentially endanger Americans in the interest of enriching a wealthy few, such as Nixon and Holifield.

In November 1974, *Ramparts* published an essay titled "The Southwest: America's New Appalachia," contributed by Thomas Brom, who was an investigative writer for the Community Ownership Organizing Project in Oakland, California. He described the "New Appalachia" as the territory stretching across the Colorado Plateau to the Mexican border. He noted that while Appalachia was colonized by the steel companies looking for a dependable supply of coking coal, the Southwest was being systemically invaded by mining and utilities companies eager to exploit the vast reserves of low-sulfur "steam" coal for regional power plants. And although the regional developers rarely used the word "colony," what was happening to the area was, Brom asserted, "an open secret."[135]

This industry was, he explained, heavily capital intensive, and the Southwest was

---

[135] Thomas Brom, "The Southwest: America's New Appalachia," *Ramparts Magazine*, November 1974, p. 17.

dependent on outside supplies of capital for the mining of these primary goods. The result was relatively fewer jobs per dollar invested, and income leakages (in the form of profits and dividends) out of the region. U.S. industry and government alike avoided the Third World analogy when dealing with exploitation of Indian resources, but the Indian tribes themselves were, Brom noted, savvy enough to make the connection. The Northern Cheyenne in Montana and North Dakota, for example, sued the Bureau of Indian affairs to force termination of all existing coal permits and leases on what remained of their tribal lands. "With good lawyers and hard bargaining," Brom wrote, the Indians of the western states could gain a piece of the development profits. They could also gain more than just short-term dollars from royalties and a few jobs. But they would, he explained, still inhabit an energy colony, forever changed from the land they inherited. "None of us—Indians, Anglos, and

Chicanes alike," he lamented, would "ever again see the Southwest" as it had "existed for centuries." But who owned and who controlled the coal and the water, Brom concluded, and the power and gasification plants of the Southwest would make a tremendous difference. It could, he believed, be the difference between an "energy graveyard sucked dry" by the cities that surrounded it, and an energy colony that developed some autonomy and secondary industry through local control.[136]

In the final analysis the population bomb that seemed to be so dire in the early 1970s was temporarily abated. Also, the federal and many state governments did, in fact, grow more, albeit often reluctantly, invested in recycling initiatives in the waning decades of the twentieth century. In some ways, the articles that comprised the body of this chapter seemed dated, but others are shockingly

---

[136] Ibid, p. 20.

prescient and requisite. Many of the dire problems and predictions broached in *Ramparts* in the late-1960s and early 1970s, for example, remained pressing issues well into the twenty-first century, especially manmade global warming, which has gotten significantly worse since the end of the Vietnam war and subsequent globalization industrialization of countries such as China, India, and Vietnam. The collapse of the Soviet Union and the end of the Cold War ultimately opened new vistas and markets for capitalist exploitation and development, which led to even more poverty and destruction of the environment in service of the global economy. And one of the two major political parties in the United States, which had the most powerful economy in the world, routinely denied that global warming was manmade, which was an obvious and shameless excuse to ensure that business as usual continued unfettered, which has had created dire consequences for the future of the world's ecosystem and life. Fossil fuel industry-insiders were also routinely put in charge of agencies such as the Environmental Protection Agency, which were designed to curb the most pernicious aspects of capitalist development, thus ensuring that profits remained a greater priority than human life. And so, instead of protecting the environment, these industry insiders in fact worked systemically to dismantle the very protective agencies that had been designed to check the most rapacious excesses of economic development on the natural world, including human life. In other words, much like all other aspects of the civil rights revolution of the 1960s and 1970s, those movements making great strides were often pushed back into place in the waning decades of the twentieth century and early decades of the twenty-first century in order to make way for more economic development at the expense of basic human rights. In that sense, the world needs a

Ramparts Magazine much as it did during the Vietnam War Era/Civil Rights Revolution chapter in American history.

CHAPTER EIGHT

"The Counterculture"

The counterculture was at the forefront of advocating the right to live a safe, healthy, and happy existence outside of the mainstream, which in America was increasingly associated with neoliberal capitalism, unsustainable industrial development, warfare, militarism, racism, sexism, evangelicalism, and political conservatism. *Ramparts Magazine* championed the counterculture, which it was also a conspicuous and prominent voice of. *Ramparts* was by the 1967 "summer of Love" headquartered in San Francisco. The Bay Area was an epicenter of the countercultural movement of the late-1960s through early 1970s.

This chapter thus begins with a review of *Ramparts'* essays about the culture, economics, and politics of the Bay Area, most notably Oakland, which was the birthplace of the Black Panther Party. The focus of the chapter then fixes on the magazine's articles about drugs, most notably LSD. The focus then shifts to *Ramparts'* depiction of hippies. *Ramparts* also published a handful of articles about communal living. The section on communal living is followed by a review of *Ramparts'* articles pertaining to gay liberation, which grew especially prominent in the late 1960s – early 1970s after the 1969 Stonewall Riot in lower Manhattan. The section on gay liberation dovetails with rock and roll, which went through radical changes in the 1960s and 1970s, changes which mirrored larger currents in the nation and the New Left. For example, in the early 1960s folk-rock musician Bob Dylan was the troubadour of the New Left. But by the time the magazine finally folded in the summer of 1975 Dylan had long since gone electric, gotten addicted to cocaine, and removed himself from the public eye and the movements that he was made a talisman for during the Sixties. The voice of the New Left by 1975 was, what was left of it anyway, was more likely androgynous British musicians such as David Bowie and Lou Reed. Other influential rock musicians such as Janis Joplin, Jimi Hendrix, and Jim Morrison had died. At times the magazine, as illuminated by the final section of this chapter, seemed to express the spirit of *The Anarchist Cookbook* (1971). As such, the last section of this chapter examines *Ramparts'* penchant for "sticking it to the man," as it were, paying specific attention to articles that seemed meant to antagonize the editors' perceived enemies – the conservative squares on the right of the political spectrum who were not hep to the counterculture, namely corporations, politicians, and law enforcement agencies.

The Bay Area

As mentioned above, the Bay Area, which included Oakland, San Francisco, and Berkeley, California was *Ramparts'* home turf from the end of the Johnson administration through the end of Nixon's term. The magazine was both influenced by and an influencer of the counterculture that blossomed in the Bay Area in the late-1960s. But even before the magazine moved its headquarters from suburban southern California to metropolitan San Francisco the editors of the publication kept a watchful eye on events in the area. In May 1965, for instance, *Ramparts* published a letter written by a resident of Berkeley named Dr. Neal Blumenfeld, M.D. The letter was titled by the *Ramparts* editors as "The Psychology of Berkeley." In it, Blumenfeld asserted that the University of California could potentially be invigorated by what he perceived to be the "moral struggle" at the root of the Free Speech

Movement that had rocked that campus in the 1964-64 school year.[137]

In February 1966, eight months before the official founding of the Black Panther Party, *Ramparts* published a twenty-five page editorial titled "Metropoly: The Story of Oakland, California" that both foreshadowed the Bay Area's exorbitant real estate prices. Oakland was in 1966 a city with 380,000 inhabitants, which made it the second largest industrial city in the United States. It was also an epicenter of the counterculture. The editors of *Ramparts* provided an analogy of Oakland as the board in a faux boardgame called "Metropoly." Oakland was, however, the editors explained, but one version of "Metropoly" that could also be played by anyone living in any American city with a population of a quarter-million inhabitants or

---

[137] Neal Blumenfeld, M.D., "Letters: The Psychology of Berkeley," *Ramparts Magazine*, May 1965, p. 15.

more. The tragedy of Oakland was, in short, not just regional; it was also a national tragedy. The object of "Metropoly" was survival, and the obstacles were chronic unemployment, racial imbalance, cultural deprivation, economic strangulation, educational disparity, housing inadequacy, entrenched power versus poverty, stultifying bureaucracy, and loss of identity. These were also the parameters by which the editors structured the essay, which touched on themes as diverse as the Hell's Angel's biker gang, which was a product of the city; beat poet Allen Ginsberg who said that Oakland was "paranoid" and in dire need of a "soul cleansing;" and the city fathers who controlled the city's real estate industry and law enforcement agencies.[138] The rules for playing "Metropoly" in Oakland, the editors wrote, were simple: If one were among the substandard-earning income families that

---

[138] *Ramparts* editorial staff, *"The Story of Oakland, California,"* Ramparts Magazine, February 1966, p. 30.

comprised forty-seven percent of Oakland's population, the player of "Metropoly" waited his turn, shook the dice, counted his spaces and kept quiet. He also went to jail when he was told to, and only passed "Go" when he received permission. He paid his taxes. And above all, he did not "rock the boat." The rules were, however, far laxer if the player was one of the elite group that made ninety-nine percent of the decisions in Oakland. "After all," the editors wrote, those elite players knew the bankers. And since the other players constantly had to land on elite players' property, the rents they paid made it far more difficult to buy any houses or hotels themselves. This analogy, the editors demonstrated in the essay, applied with dismaying exactitude to life in Oakland, where the game of "Metropoly" was "being played on a scale slightly below the epic."[139]

---

[139] Ibid, pp. 25-26.

And out of the mud of Oakland flowered the counterculture. The editors depicted Oakland and fast becoming what city fathers feared most – an inevitable "explosion from the ghetto within, and an invasion of 'outside agitators' from the sprawling, adjacent Berkeley campus of the University of California. Both fears were, the editors explained, combined in the previous year when the Berkeley Vietnam Day Committee (VDC) scheduled an anti-war march from the campus through Berkeley and on through the Oakland ghetto, which provoked a confrontation that the editors of *Ramparts* believed illuminated "the tinderbox condition of the great Oakland ghetto and the cantankerous, running-scared mentality of the city's leaders."[140] Oakland thus needed more than federal largesse to recover economically, socially, and politically, the editors declared. It

---

[140] Ibid, p. 27.

needed a total revitalization and redefinition of itself as a heterogeneous community. And this rebirth could, they asserted, only come, "as the Phoenix, from the ashes of the ghetto." Only such a revolutionary awakening, they concluded, stirring in the slums and accepted in the hills, could save Oakland from the deepening and eventually disastrous war between its two worlds – rich and poor and black and white. Despite the singular obtuseness of its public officials, Oakland, the editors asserted, was not unique. "It was America — it was the American core city." Oakland might be "a funny place," they conceded, "but the joke" was on all Americans.[141] The editors concluded the essay by elaborating that local law enforcement agencies had responded to the rising discontent and militancy of the college students and amongst the city's most indigent

---

[141] Ibid, p. 50.

by increasingly militarizing its police force. In short, poor Americans in cities like Oakland were increasingly reacting to the dire circumstances of poverty and lack of equality in the Affluent Society. The elites' subsequent reaction was not substantive social and economic reform, but rather the militarization of law enforcement at a moment in history when groups such as the inchoate Black Panthers were finding common cause with anti-colonialist movements in Africa, Latin America, and Asia, as well as creating tenuous alliances with middle class college students.

In August 1969, a little more than two months after what came to be known as "Bloody Thursday," *Ramparts* published a piece titled "A Photographic Essay of the People's Park" contributed by Dugald Stermer which chronicled a plot of land owned by the University of California at Berkeley, but appropriated by a cadre of leftists to be an all-inclusive community gathering place. The park came to be a symbol between the counterculture and the hegemonic culture they rebelled against. Much like camps set up by the more recent Occupy Movement in Wall Street in the twenty-first century, People's Park became a symbol of opposition towards the political establishment. The Berkeley community park was set up at a time when the university was a hotbed for counterculture movements and anti-war protest. Stermer's essay chronicled the early history of the park, but most ink was dedicated to the events of May 15, 1969. Three years earlier, Ronald Reagan's gubernatorial campaign vowed to clean up what he considered to be the mess at Berkeley, referring to the Free Speech Movement and the counterculture that blossomed out of it on that campus amongst both students and faculty. The events of Bloody Thursday followed days of tension as rumors spread that the university would attempt to reclaim the People's Park area.

Reagan authorized law enforcement, which included combined forces of the Berkeley police, the California Highway Patrol, and the Alameda County Sheriff's Department, to use any means necessary in their eviction of park inhabitants. Thousands of protesters had gathered in the park on May 15, 1969, when police opened fire with shotguns and buckshot. Student James Rector, who was 25-years-old, died from police gunshot wounds, while another man was blinded in the chaos that unfolded near Telegraph Avenue. *Lines of soldiers with fixed bayonets and California Highway Patrolmen also prevented the demonstrators from moving off the campus towards city hall.* More than 400 protesters were ultimately arrested. In the days following Bloody Thursday, riot police and helicopter tear gas were used as crowd control. *It seemed to many that the Vietnam War was coming home to roost.*

"A Photographic Essay of the People's Park" was followed in the August 1969 edition of *Ramparts* by an essay titled "The Dialectics of Confrontation: Who Ripped Off The Park? The Battle of Berkeley" written by Robert Scheer. He reported that the identity and movements of what he referred to as a "death squad" of Alameda County Deputy Sheriffs, which, as it moved in a circular path through the area of protest, used its shotguns to cause almost all the serious injuries as well as the death of Rector. "Reagan was pleased," Scheer wrote, with the development of what he referred to as a "war," and that the future President of the United States was now "firmly in charge," as if he were the dictator of California. Scheer concluded by quoting Cal Berkeley Regent Fred Dutton, who Scheer believed best summarized the whole People's Park affair when he said after the Board of Regents' vote to build student housing atop People's Park: "This Board offered repression and no solutions," Dutton said. "The center keeps shrinking, and we are the provocateurs."[142]

Drugs

Ramparts also published a handful stories about drugs, most especially LSD. The first such article was published in April 1966. It was titled "LSD: The Acid Test" contributed by Donovan Bess, which was published before the drug had been made schedule-1. Bess described taking LSD-25 as the most radical way to explore what he referred to as "inner space," which was, he asserted, "as revolutionary as exploring outer space."[143] The essay used many case studies, anecdotes, quotes, and experiences to encourage readers to try the drug in a safe setting. If one were to do so, the results could be nothing short of a

---

[142] Robert Scheer, "The Dialectics of Confrontation: Who Ripped Off The Park? The Battle of Berkeley," *Ramparts Magazine*, August 1969, p. 53.

[143] Donovan Bess, "LSD: The Acid Test," *Ramparts Magazine*, April 1966, p. 42.

personal revolution of the heart and mind at the core of one's being. The purpose behind these experiments, Bess wrote, was to "find the humanity they were cheated of by ersatz education, electronic conditioning, and living in families led by synthetic productions labeled 'mother' and 'father.'"[144]

In August 1966, *Ramparts* published a colloquial account contributed by Donald Figg titled "What Uncle Sam Doesn't Know" in which he described a time when he ended up at an Army recruiting office on a head full of LSD. The upshot was that the recruiter treated him as though he were a patriotic, hawkish, and gung-ho square, when in reality he was the opposite of what the recruiter which he pejoratively referred to as "Uncle Sam" hoped he was.

---

[144] Ibid, p. 43.

In November 1966, *Ramparts* published an editorial contributed by Paul Krassner titled "Press: Genesis (Acid and *EVO*)." Krassner described the *East Village Other* (which is now *The Village Voice*) as taking its inspiration from LSD-researcher Timothy Leary. *EVO* had recently published a banner headline, "America Hates Her Crazies!" with the rest of page one being taken up by photos of "the unholy trinity," which included Timothy Leary, Ralph Ginzburg, and Allen Ginsberg, along with a notice saying "Wanted by the FBI;" a lot of faux fingerprints and J. Edgar Hoover's signature reproduced from an official Wanted flyer.[145] And so it came to pass that two FBI men visited the *EVO* office. Though the editors were let off with a warning, the FBI confiscated the last 3,000 copies still on newsstands.

---

[145] Paul Krassner, "Press: Genesis (Acid and *EVO*)," *Ramparts Magazine*, November 1966, p. 62.

In November 1967, *Ramparts* published a pictorial essay titled "Jail Notebook" contributed by Ken Kesey, the author of *One Flew Over the Cuckoo's Nest* (1962). Kesey's essay included excerpts from the journal he filled as an inmate in San Mateo, California in 1967. The original charge against Kesey was possessing four roaches of Marijuana joints which, he said, were likely brought to his home and planted by one of the sixteen deputy sheriffs who raided it after complaints by his influential neighbors against the excessive joy he had allowed his friends to demonstrate in the backyard, as they investigated the properties of LSD. Kesey was very well-known amongst both hippies and law enforcement agencies for hosting acid tests in and around the Bay Area of Northern California. He kept a notebook in his prison barracks locker and in the evenings filled it with spastic, pyrotechnic, color-drunk essays done with a watchmaker's precision, to show how much the world was worth loving anyway. When words came into the notebook, they revealed some of his deep sadness about the moral state of the Unites States and his hatred, not for people, but for the violent and repressive nature of the empire.

Ramparts published another essay contributed by Krassner in January 1970 titled "LSD and SDS, and Little Lambs Eat Ivy." Krassner explained the point and purpose of the recently created cultural alliance of acid-friendly leftists dubbed the Movement Speakers Bureau. Many activists, he explained, had accepted speaking engagements at universities and elsewhere through booking agencies that received thirty to forty percent of the fee. Others had wanted to speak before college audiences to raise money for projects, but did not have the necessary contacts. The Movement Speakers Bureau was thus created to correct that situation. The MSB was, Krassner noted, to be run by movement people for the benefit of movements associated with the New Left. All of the profits would thus be dispersed among a variety of organizations at the end of each year, to be decided on a one-man one-vote basis. The advisory board included Dave Dellinger, Allen Ginsberg, Dick Gregory, Tom Hayden, William Kunstler and Bobby Seale.

Hippies

As the reader might expect from the very positive portrayal of LSD and LSD explorers, *Ramparts* also published a handful of essays depicting hippies in a non-pejorative light, which was very much unlike the mainstream American media, which tended to depict hippies as naïve, grubby, unwashed, and overly idealistic nincompoops. That said, many editors and contributors to *Ramparts* chafed at many hippie's embrace of Timothy Leary's edict to "drop out" of the political scene and revolutionary movement. Whereas hippies seemed more concerned with exploring inner space, *Ramparts* was a muckraking publication dedicated to exposing corruption in and ultimately changing American institutions. In January 1967, for example, *Ramparts* published an article titled "Manners and Morals" contributed by Ralph J. Gleason, which offered anecdotes and case studies to illuminate that long hair had become a curios and odd cultural wedge between members of the counterculture and the militarists, political figures, law enforcement agencies, and corporate executives they sought to be the antithesis of. For instance, Gleason noted that J. Edgar Hoover, a closeted homosexual, associated long hair on men as being associated with criminality. Many young men, meanwhile, grew their hair long as a means of consciously demarking themselves from authoritarian white men such as Hoover.

In March 1967 *Ramparts* published a lengthy essay titled "The Social History of the

Hippies" contributed by Warren Hinckle. It included several images of the "dramatis personae" of the American "hippie scene" including Kesey, Ginsberg, Leary, the Diggers, and venues and/or events that were considered gathering places for hippies, such as the Fillmore, the Psychedelic Circus, and the Human Be In. Hinckle described Ginsberg as "the elder statesmen of America's synthetic gypsy movement."[146] Hippies were many things, Hinckle explained, but most prominently the bearded and beaded inhabitants of the Haight-Ashbury, which he described as a "little psychedelic city-state edging Golden Gate Park" were folks who wanted nothing to do with America's corporatist, racist, sexist, and anti-democratic imperialism.

---

[146] Warren Hinckle, "The Social History of the Hippies," *Ramparts Magazine*, March 1967, p. 5.

He described Leary, Ginsberg, and Kesey as "ghosts of hippies past." The younger hippies, Hinckle noted, talked about reducing governmental controls, the sanctity of the individual, and the need for equality among men. They also talked, very seriously, about the kind of society they wanted to live in, and the fact that if they wanted an ideal world they would have to go out and make it for themselves, because nobody, least of all the government, was going to do it for them. The younger hippies, Hinckle elaborated, had a clear vision of the ideal community — a psychedelic community, to be sure — where everyone was turned on and beautiful and loving and happy and floating free. Hippies also, he asserted, represented a radical political philosophy: communal life, drastic restriction of private property, rejection of violence, creativity before consumption, freedom before authority, and a de-emphasis of government and traditional forms of leadership. Despite a disturbing tendency to quietism, all hippies ipso facto had, whether they believed it or not, a political posture—one of unremitting opposition to the Establishment which insisted on branding them criminals because they enjoyed LSD and marijuana, and hated them anyway, because they enjoyed sleeping nine in a room and three to a bed, seemed to have free sex and guiltless minds, and could raise healthy children in dirty clothes.

The hippie choice of weapons was, Hinckle explained, to love the Establishment to death rather than protest it or blow it up. Hippies, he noted, also possessed what he referred to as "a confounding disconcern about traditional political methods or issues." The mainstream media often depicted them in bright baggy clothes and skipping jump rope, but hippies were, in fact, Hinckle wrote, as serious about what they were doing as the John Birch Society or the Junior League was.[147]

---

[147] Ibid, p. 10.

Hinckle, however, did not believe that the Haight-Ashbury represented anything near a utopia. He considered the droves of kids coming to San Francisco in the winter of 1967 to be a psychedelic "Grapes of Wrath." These kids were often lured to Haight-Ashbury by what he referred to as "hippie merchants" who created the notion of utopia to sell products. These hippie merchants had created what Hinckle deemed to be a mess that these merchants would not be able to resolve, nor would they want to because it was in their material interest not to. These hippie merchants, in short, were destroying the real political potential of the movement by commoditizing it as a dream of finding wavy gravy enlightenment by simply turning on and dropping out from society. The danger in the hippie movement was, Hinckle concluded, more than overcrowded streets and possible hunger riots. If more and more youngsters began to share the hippie political posture of unrelenting quietism, the future of activist, serious politics was, he presciently declared, bound to be adversely affected. The hippies, he concluded, had shown that it could be very pleasant to drop out of the arduous task of attempting to steer a difficult, unrewarding society towards the ideals it supposedly represented. But when that was done, he warned, you left the driving to madmen such the Hell's Angels.[148]

In August 1969, *Ramparts* published an essay titled "Living" written by Joan Holden and R.G. Davis. They expressed frustration with Julian Beck and Judith Malina, the founders of the Living Theater in New York City. The Living Theater, Holden and Davis explained, was the original radical theater, challenging the assumptions of the system while the rest of the avant-garde was

---

[148] Ibid, p. 26.

worried about metaphysics or McCarthyism. The Living Theater had been in exile for five years, "a wandering religious community" comprised of 35 people, at least two of them geniuses, living in an atmosphere, the legend went, of the most fervent intensity, suffering, tripping, and creating as one. But the wisdom it brought back from that abyss, snatched from the jaws of hell, turned out to be — "turn on, tune in, drop out." There was thus a simple lesson about the Living Theater's move from radical politics to the collective's escape from revolutionary politics, Davis and Holden argued, that helped illuminate a "significant bit of cultural history."[149] In the 1950s the avant-garde mirrored suffering; but by 1969 it credited itself with having made a revolutionary change in proclaiming joy. But no movement that focused on the repressed or released individual, Holden and Davis

---

[149] Joan Holden and R.G. Davis, "Living," *Ramparts Magazine*, August 1969, p. 62.

concluded, was ever going to threaten a system such as consumer capitalism that was based on individualism. The concern of the vanguard was not awareness, but action; not to change consciousness but to change institutions. "We don't care if you keep your parts private," Holden and Davis concluded, "just make your property public."[150]

In December 1969, *Ramparts* published a cute story titled "Inside the Great Pigasus Plot" contributed by Jerry Rubin, a Yippie leader who was a master of getting free publicity. The essay was an excerpt from Rubin's book *DO IT!: Scenarios of the Revolution* (1970), which had not yet been published. Rubin, Abbie Hoffman, and others brought the New York Stock Exchange to a halt by tossing money into the air and watched gleefully as the stockbrokers scrambled to fetch the bills from the floor. Later, during the Presidential elections of 1968 the Youth International Party, a guerilla theater

---

[150] Ibid, p. 65.

troupe, nominated their own candidate for the presidency.

The nominee was dubbed Pigasus the Immortal, a 145-pound pig that they felt was a realistic alternative to Richard Nixon, George Wallace and Hubert Humphrey. Rubin promised, on behalf of Pigasus, a fair election campaign and if Pigasus won the election he would be eaten. This would, Rubin joked, reverse the usual democratic process in which the pig was elected and proceeded to eat the people. The campaign slogan was "Why take half a hog when you can have the whole hog?"[151] Rubin's essay was published a few months after he and seven others had been charged by the federal government on charges of conspiracy to incite the police riot that broke out at the Democratic National Convention in Chicago in the summer of 1968. "With my

---

[151] Jerry Rubin, "Inside the Great Pigasus Plot," *Ramparts Magazine*, December 1969, p. 11.

indictment," he wrote, "I join the host of outstanding world figures who have crossed state lines to create civil disturbance: the Beatles, Elvis Presley, the late Marilyn Monroe, Jim Morrison, the president of the United States and Joe Namath. And you know who else is guilty?" he rhetorically asked readers. "The hippies who dressed in psychedelic Indian clothes, boarded British ships and threw tea overboard in 1773!"[152] He explained the paradox of his situation in legal terms: "If your speech is ineffective, it is protected by the Constitution," he wrote. "If your speech is effective, you are 'inciting to riot.'" Effective speech — speech that moved people — was, he explained, "against the law."[153] Rubin's essay concluded by soliciting funds for the legal defense of "The Conspiracy" — on trial in

---

[152] Ibid, p. 18.

[153] Ibid, p. 18.

Chicago for their part in the demonstrations during the 1968 Democratic convention.

Rubin's article was followed in the December 1969 edition of *Ramparts* by an essay titled "Shooting Up a Rock Bonanza" contributed by Joan Holden, who was a member of the San Francisco Mime Troupe. Like Hinckle, Holden very much regretted the commercialization of the hippie movement, which she likewise perceived to be as an undermining force in the movement. The summer of 1969 was, she explained, the lamentable moment in world history when what was once known as the "be-in" turned into that "cash crop called the rock festival." The 450,000 at the Woodstock Music and Art Fair, the mammoth "Aquarian Age Exhibition" that provoked a special issue of *Life* seemed to think that the new age had indeed arrived.

Holden, however, sounded a cautionary note by reminding readers that when Abbie Hoffman grabbed the microphone and told the

Woodstock crowd that their numbers meant nothing unless they could free John Sinclair (a Detroit street leader serving ten years on a pot charge), Pete Townshend of the English group The Who, who was also onstage, clubbed Hoffman over the head with his electric guitar. The movement had been split, Holden argued, between those who saw no conflict between "serving the community" concomitant to getting rich, and those who saw a definite contradiction in such capitalist profiteering of the counterculture.[154] These cash cows known as rock festivals, Holden lamented had the unintended consequence of making apathetic hedonists of would be idealists. This "New Breed" of capitalists responsible for the rock festivals, she argued, might deny that their celebration business was a branch of the containment industry, but the older generation

---

[154] Joan Holden, "Shooting Up a Rock Bonanza," *Ramparts Magazine*, December 1969, p. 70.

seemed to be getting hip to it. "You could probably start a revolution with rock music," she concluded, "if you could get someone to outlaw it."[155]

In December 1971, *Ramparts* published an essay titled "From the Cockettes With Love and Squalor" written by Jon Stewart. The Cockettes were an avant-garde psychedelic hippie theater group founded by "Hibiscus" (George Edgerly Harris II) in the fall of 1969. The troupe was formed out of a group of hippie artists, men and women, who were living in Kaliflower, one of the many communes in the Haight-Ashbury section of San Francisco. Hibiscus came to live with them because of their preference for dressing outrageously and proposed the idea of putting their lifestyle on stage. The Cockettes, who were performing at the Fillmore East in New York City when Stewart's profile about them

---

[155] Ibid, p. 78.

was published, were, Stewart wrote, "queens with a manic sense of humor, fools in their mothers' fur coats and their fathers' buckle-up Army boots, beautiful fools, in love."[156] They also, Stewart wrote, represented the "artistic and cultural anarchy in the midst of general constipation."[157] Beyond San Francisco, New York, and Paris, Stewart lamented, there probably were not many cities that would allow them to perform, at least not the kind of blue and edgy material that they did best, and anything short of the totally outrageous would have been contrived, artificial, unnatural and consequently unfunny.

The theme of the New Left being reduced from a potent political movement to a relic of history could be detected in an essay published in the August 1971 edition of *Ramparts* titled "Jesus Now: Hogwash and

---

[156] Jon Stewart, "From the Cockettes With Love and Squalor," *Ramparts Magazine*, December 1971, pp. 52.

[157] Ibid, p. 53.

Holy Water" written by James Nolan, who was a poet from New Orleans living in Sonoma County, California. He described the rise of "Jesus Freaks" and "freak evangelism," in California in particular during the early 1970s, whom he perceived to be "a fairly new breed in the hip-liberation menagerie" and evidence of former activists growing increasingly demoralized and turning towards individualism and new age spiritual development at the expense of societal revolution and institutional reform, which the New Left especially championed through the 1960s. The message of Jesus freaks was, Nolan explained, simply down-home, Jesus-is-the-way, evangelical fundamentalism delivered with flower-child innocence and visionary fervor and was incredibly broad-based.[158]

---

[158] James Nolan, "Jesus Now: Hogwash and Holy Water," *Ramparts Magazine*, August 1971, p. 20.

The American blow-your-mind, zappo-revolutionary kids were, Nolan explained, literally flocking into the Jesus Freaks' fundamentalist conversion parlors and coming out with handfuls of psychedelic-looking tracts, a "Biblical" set of morals and "big Billy James Hargis friend-do-you-know-the-Lord grins." The Jesus houses, as he referred to them, offered kids a place to crash indefinitely, free food and free medical care, a toothbrush and comb, enough to do and more than enough to believe in; and there was also usually a "Mother or Daddy figure" who, despite the preaching and soul-saving, really seemed to care, and would not make one cut his hair. All-in-all, Nolan wrote, it was an unbeatable combination if one was 18-years-old, a runaway from some "cow town Paducah or plastic Executive Oaks," used to dropping acid by the six-pack, alone and penniless in the "ghetto-zoo, fucked-up and fucked-over, testing around for some ultimate reality trip, with nothing to do and no place in particular to do it."[159] The Jesus trip was, Nolan noted, particularly attractive to children brought up in staunchly religious homes (such as former Catholics and Baptists) or to kids reared on suburban textbook agnosticism, the ones who were lost even before they had found anything to be lost from. Most of the converted were between 14 and 20 years old, and they possessed an amazingly glowing energy and commitment, "all shining as though they had just washed their hair." Maybe the Jesus movement was, Nolan cautioned, only a later version of Love-Generation-Haight-Ashbury optimism, the flowers-and-transcendence stage of growing up American that would eventually turn the same worn path to skepticism and militancy when they reached the age of 23.

Whether the new masses of Jesus freaks were only visiting or whether they planned to

---

[159] Ibid, p. 21.

stay, they were, Nolan explained, pitching their tents very close to one of the main arteries of the American heart. Jesus freaks had, he noted, introduced only a few real variations to *Bible*-pounding, tent-revival, fundamentalist Christianity, among them street language (Jesus was no longer Lord and Savior but Leader and Liberator) and the communal lifestyle. But over-arching all else was a passionate belief that the world would end within their lifetimes while Jesus returned to rapture them off to a very literal heaven with streets of gold and angels twanging on electric-amp harps, the thought of which clouded their eyes and left them murmuring "fa-a-ar out."[160] But Nolan also noted the commercialization of Christianity amongst the Jesus freaks, thereby positing it as part-and-parcel of the capitalist system and thus the antithesis of true revolution. There were, he lamented, Honk-if-you-love-Jesus bumper-stickers, Jesus day-glo

---

[160] Ibid, p. 21.

posters, Jesus on the cover of the Whole Earth Supplement, Jesus comics, the Jesus look, *Jesus Christ, Superstar*, and Jesus rock. Jesus was, he quipped, "even more popular than John Lennon." Somehow fundamentalist evangelism had, he noted, caught up with mass media and was plastering stickers, converting rock stars and plugging in amps all over the place. As people lost their grip on the revolution, Nolan lamented, they seemed "to be grasping for absolutes." Whether the content of a Jesus freak preacher's message was hogwash or holy water did not, Nolan explained, make too much difference. Whether these evangelistic Christians were, as Nietzsche accused, predatory birds who swooped down on weak life in distress or, in a more charitable view, fanatical do-gooders with an overly developed, paternal sense, made little difference to critics such as Nolan. The fact was, he declared, these people, and the leaders of other mass movements like them, were bringing freaked-out kids down and placing them in a community situation where roles were assigned and talents encouraged. Mything-out on Jesus, though, was not, he explained, too different from spacing-out on drugs.[161]

Communal Living

In the late 1960s and early 1970s *Ramparts* published a handful of articles pertaining to communal living. The first such essay was a cautionary editorial contributed by Robert Houriet titled "Communing in Meadville" and published in late-November 1968. It chronicled a cadre of thirty-two hippies ranging in ages from 16 to 36 who had taken up residence in a small town in Pennsylvania. Most of the cadre came from middle class homes in every part of the country. Many had attended college and graduate school. Organizationally, they avoided rules and voted

---

[161] Ibid, p. 26.

on very few matters. They also shared clothes and other possessions. One of the few issues the family did vote upon was to admit curious visitors and adventuresome teenagers to visit their communal farm. It turned out to be a disastrous decision for the commune. Once the farm appeared to enough locals to be converting youth to a different style of life and thus "undermining their morals" the community bristled and drove the hippies out of the county.

    The theme of hippies in search of utopianism and that quest fast turning dystopian, which was actually quite common in *Ramparts*, continued in an essay published in the November 1969 edition of the magazine titled "Canyon: A Troubled Paradise" written by Sol Stern. He chronicled a community of artisans and professionals who cared about their land and about its hundred-year history and traditions in Contra Costa County, California, which was a 20-minute drive from the big cities of the Bay Area. The collective called their community the Canyon.

Canyonites, Stern wrote, were like people all over the country who were leaving the "boiling cauldron of the big city" and seeking the space and freedom that was promised in the American Dream. But these people were soon finding that there was about as much trouble in their would-be wooded paradise as there was in the urban dystopias they had escaped. Instead of sheriffs and shotguns, Canyonites faced a limitless coercive bureaucracy that sought to drive them from the area. Instead of armed occupation, the Canyonites faced a new version of a familiar weapon—an onslaught of Rural Renewal. The issue centered on the fact that the community was built atop a piece of unincorporated land that lacked a sewage system. The Canyonites thus devised a clever sewage disposal plan that called for the installation at every home site a cheap and portable sewage treatment plant—

aeration units that had only recently been placed on the market. The beauty of the proposed sewage system, Stern explained, was its total application to the ecological and planning needs of Canyon. It also avoided the orthodox sewage disposal methods which were being employed in the Bay Area in which untreated waste was piped directly into the ocean — a process that had led to (among other ecological disasters) the pollution of the Bay and the destruction of a once flourishing fishing industry.

The Contra Costa Board of Supervisors ultimately voted 4-to-1 against allowing the residents of Canyon to have their own sewage district, which meant the community had no sewage system, which put them in violation of myriad local ordinances. In other words, The Contra Costa Board of Supervisors killed the Canyon community because they preferred the land to be developed for commercial use rather than communal living inhabited by progressive artists and intellectuals. Canyon was not comprised of missionaries, Stern conceded. But if there was anything that they wanted people to learn from their community, it was that it was imperative that Americans "stopped tearing up and exploiting the greatest gift bestowed on them, the land, and instead really start living on it."[162]

In August 1971, *Ramparts* published an account of the attempts of Rainbow Farm, a commune on the Eastern seaboard, to get themselves through the harsh winter months and the early stages of their life together. Because of the widespread interest in rural life and alternative lifestyles, *Ramparts* opted to devote more space in the early 1970s to alternative lifestyles. The picture painted, however, is most often bleak, depicting people living at the margins of society in the richest nation in the world, metaphysically nourished

---

[162] Sol Stern, "Canyon: A Troubled Paradise," *Ramparts Magazine*, November 1969, p. 28.

by a sense of righteousness and idealism more so than food. The residents of rainbow Farm were, however, also depicted as being full of joy, love, optimism, and hope. "We're neither political heroes nor rugged vagabonds," the anonymous resident of the farm wrote in his editorial, "famous farmers nor foot-loose freaks." They were simply a collection or folks of various ages, education and social backgrounds, that ached to live sustainably, responsibly, and removed from the larger society, which they perceived to be obsessed with war and materialism.

Ramparts published another communiqué in September 1971 that had made its way from Rainbow Farm. It chronicled a day in the mostly monotonous life of the resident of the farm, who described a daily existence much like a person raising a family in the suburbs, replete with brothers fighting over who would clean up a spill, etc. The primary difference in the social experience of those living on Rainbow Farm was, however, that rather than being cloistered in a suburban gated community, the family was living with dozens of others with their own energy fields, hang-ups, etc.

The third installment of the "Notes from Rainbow Farm" was published in the December 1971 edition of *Ramparts*. It was the most personal entry yet published. The writer explained his dream and his crush on a "dreamy" and "witch-like" painter named Blyth, who had lived at Rainbow Farm since it began. The article provided a unique insight into the mind of an anonymous man living on an anonymous commune somewhere on the east coast of the United States.

The final article explicitly about communal living *Ramparts* published appeared in the October 1974 edition of the magazine. It was a review of Michael Weiss' *Living Together: A Year in the Life of a City Commune* contributed by Andrew Kopkind. Weiss' book was about a small group of young, educated people (a journalist, an archaeologist, a physician, a teacher, a medical student, a community organizer, a therapist, and a microbiologist) who in the summer of 1971 decided to upend their middle class lives by joining together to live communally in Philadelphia, Pennsylvania. Caught up in the political and cultural furor of their times, dissatisfied as so many of their contemporaries were with the contradictions between their political and social values and their daily lives, they decided to experiment with sharing their incomes, possessions, household chores and most importantly, some measure of themselves.

After living together for a year, Weiss, his wife Ruth, their young son Matt, and six other people realized what almost every intentional communalist also discovered: that communal living in a society that shaped people to think of themselves as individuals first and members of a community second was hard-pressed to survive very long.[163] In other words, communes, Kopkind argued, rarely ended up being the social utopias communards hoped they would be. He advised other communards to make space to be themselves as well as part of the larger community they lived amongst. Shared interests and responsibilities were also, he noted, a kind of glue that kept communes together, alive and thriving. A lack of shared interests would also likely spell doom for communes.

Gay Liberation

An often overlooked or ignored aspect of the American counterculture of the 1960s – 1970s was the increased openness and activism of homosexuals in the realm of revolutionary politics. Though *Ramparts* likewise gave short-shrift to gay liberation politics compared to other intertwined movements associated with

---

[163] Andrew Kopkind, "Communes: The Way We Lived Then," *Ramparts Magazine*, October 1974, p. 51.

the counterculture such as the quest for civil rights amongst African Americans, Native Americans, Mexican Americans, and women, the magazine did publish four essays in the early 1970s relating to homosexuality in the sphere of politics and popular culture. The first such article was a profile published in October 1971 written by Jon Stewart titled "Charles Pierce: Female Impersonator as Culture Hero(ine)" about a loveable, popular, and iconic drag queen who, Stewart wrote, was "without qualification, the most professional, talented, successful popular entertainer to hit the city since George Murphy's last hurrah." Pierce's show was, Stewart gushed, "a unique blend of high camp, high drag" and "nostalgia, which, in his recent performances, went straight to the heart of San Francisco's preoccupation with its own decadence."[164]

---

[164] Jon Stewart, "Charles Pierce: Female Impersonator as Culture Hero(ine)," *Ramparts Magazine*, October 1971, p. 60.

In November 1971, *Ramparts* published an essay titled "Out of the Closet: A Gay Manifesto" written by Allen Young, who had been active in the gay liberation movement in New York since early 1970. Most of the ideas expressed in the essay, Young wrote, were the result of a collective process, involving many "gay sisters and brothers" who had engaged him in struggle and had identified with the New Left for several years. He made a note of explaining that there was no monolithic meaning to being gay and that he was only speaking for himself. "Gay, in its most far-reaching sense," he explained, meant "not homosexual, but sexually free…" It was sexual freedom premised upon the notion of pleasure through equality, not pleasure where there was inequality. As gays, he declared, "we demand an end to the gender programming which starts when we are born (pink for girls, blue for boys)."[165] He explained that gay people were committed to building liberated communal situations where children could grow strong and free. Straights who were "threatened by us like to accuse us of separatism, " he wrote, "but our understanding of sexism is premised on the idea that in the free society everyone will be free of sex-determined roles, i.e., gay."[166]

He explained that gay liberation "consciousness raising groups" were trying to step outside the "straight man's myths and institutions," and "to suspend the limited ways" gay men tended to deal with each other, "and experiment with new ways of relating." They were men, he noted, who were struggling with their eagerness to dominate and ego-trip by being aware of the needs of others in the group, he concluded, and struggling with their tendency to intellectualize by speaking from

---

[165] Allen Young, "Out of the Closet: A Gay Manifesto," *Ramparts Magazine*, November 1971, p. 52.

[166] Ibid, p. 59.

their experiences. "We are also learning what has been forbidden us," he concluded, "to relate to one another with respect and love."[167]

In March 1973, *Ramparts* published an essay titled "Gay Rock: The Boys in the Band" written by Andrew Kopkind that profiled The Velvet Underground's Lou Reed and David Bowie, who had recently released "The Rise and Fall of Ziggy Stardust and the Spiders from Mars." Bowie and Reed were, Kopkind lamented, not really able to be truly revolutionary artists because they lived in a non-revolutionary society. "There can't be liberated people in a repressive society: only people working on liberation," Kopkind wrote. Bowie's showbiz paraphernalia and Reed's Velvety camp were, he concluded, "understandable evasions and justifiable

---

[167] Ibid, p. 59.

responses to an intolerable sexual straitjacket — but evasions and responses just the same."[168]

In December 1973, *Ramparts* published an essay titled "The Third Sex: Hold On, It's Coming" written by Nolan. He personified "A Real Man" as Norman Mailer: the booze-belting, swaggering, *Sports Illustrated* macho American male, who knew what a woman needed and how to give it to her, whether she wanted it or not. In the opposite corner, wearing a tight black mini-skirt, sat Germaine Greer, who Nolan described as possessing "the street-corner honesty of a cabbie, the erudition of a scholar, and the exuberant femininity of an Elizabethan barmaid who artfully dodged the pat on the ass she had been asking for all evening -- A Real Woman." In the third corner, wearing a lavender jumpsuit, sat what Nolan referred to as "the new American Gay: proud but martyred, surrounded by constant support

---

[168] Andrew Kopkind, "Gay Rock: The Boys in the Band," *Ramparts Magazine*, March 1973, p. 51.

but painfully alone, with the same blank look of resignation on his face as when the overhead lights in the bar slashed on to announce take-it-home-or-leave-it closing time -- The Real Outsider." The third sex, Nolan gleefully declared, was finally here.[169]

Rock-and-Roll

The editors of *Ramparts* often depicted rock-and-roll as quintessentially American and having both revolutionary and counter-revolutionary potential. Early in the history of the magazine Bob Dylan was depicted as the pied piper of folk rock and as the moral voice and talisman of the New Left. For example, in April 1965 *Ramparts* published an essay titled "The Times They are A-Changin'" contributed by Ralph J. Gleason, who was noted jazz and social critic, nationally syndicated columnist,

---

[169] James Nolan, "The Third Sex: Hold On, It's Coming," *Ramparts Magazine*, December 1973, p. 59.

and author of books on music who resided in Berkeley, California. Joan Baez and Bob Dylan, he explained, were the two leading figures in a crusade for a New Morality. They helped provide the soundtrack for the idealists of entire generation. As a result, America's young formed the basis of the counterculture and were at the forefront of America's rights revolution in the 1960s.

Gleason's essay was followed in the April 1965 edition of *Ramparts* by an article titled "We Shall Overcome" contributed by Helen Nestor and Michael Alexander, who argued that folk singers lead the student rebels during the Free Speech Movement at the University of California in 1964. The demonstration was, Nestor and Alexander argued, the social philosophy of folk singers set in action. The essayists thus argued that the action at Berkeley was linked with the songs that inspired the students. Dylan, Baez and the other "conscience singers" represented the

"New Morality" and they were the New Moralists who were "revising the priorities of the entire society." They were "simplistic" and "evangelical visionaries" who declared the "virtues are Love and Truth and Beauty" and the "ultimate sins" were to hurt another human, to break trust and not to love." The times, Nestor and Alexander concluded, were a-changin' and these young artists were among the reasons for that change.[170]

In March 1966, *Ramparts* published another article, a cover story, contributed by Gleason titled "Bob Dylan: The Children's Crusade." It included black and white illustrations of Dylan by Gene Holtan in which the folk-rock musician held a lance under his arm while riding a white steed. "Dylan's songs and lyrics changed my life because they provided a new, non-ideological basis for an attack upon the evils of our society that is

---

[170] Helen Nestor and Michael Alexander, "We Shall Overcome," *Ramparts Magazine*, April 1965, p. 48.

linked with the attacks made by other artists but which is," Gleason wrote, "because of his song and because of his youth, particularly effective." What Gleason referred to as "flashing images" embedded in Dylan's lyrics seemed to Gleason to provide "a more serious assault on the structure of the Great Society and upon its hypocrisies and pretentions than any ideology or armed might of a foreign power." America's Youth, he gushed, had "found its own way, a veritable children's crusade" led by a slender 24-year-old songwriter, singer and electric guitar player whose song royalties for the first half of 1965 were greater than the combined royalties for that same period of the celebrated Tin Pan Alley heroes. Dylan was, Gleason explained, telling the American audience (and through that audience telling the world) that it was better to make love than to make war, that the only loyalty was to oneself ('that it was not he or she or them or it that you belong to'), that politics were irrelevant ('you say 'nothin's perfect' and I tell you again there are no politics'), that the leadership cult of the Great Society was a fraud ('don't follow leaders, watch the parkin' meters'), that the old-fashioned virtues of hard work and thrift and a clean tongue were obsolete ('money doesn't talk it swears; obscenity who really cares?'). Dylan was, in short, Gleason declared, saying that the entire system of Western society, built upon Aristotelian logic, the Judeo-Christian ethic and upon a series of economic systems from Hobbes to Marx to Keynes, did not work. [171]

In October 1967, *Ramparts* published a pictorial essay titled "John Lennon Murders World War II" contributed by Stephen Schneck, who profiled the Richard Lester-John Lennon dark comedy, *How I Won The War* (1966). The plot was as follows: Lieutenant

---

[171] Ralph J. Gleason, "Bob Dylan: The Children's Crusade," *Ramparts Magazine*, March 1966, p. 27.

Goodbody (Michael Crawford), was an inept, idealistic, naïve, and almost relentlessly jingoistic wartime-commissioned (not regular) officer. One of the most subversive themes in the film was the platoon's repeated attempts or temptations to kill or otherwise rid themselves of their complete liability of the gung-ho commander. Every time a character was killed in the film he was replaced by an actor in bright red, blue, or green-colored World War II uniform, whose face was also colored and obscured so that he appeared to be a living toy soldier.

This reinforced Goodbody's repeated comparisons of war to playing a game. The mythology of modern war, Schneck wrote, was essentially a motion picture mythology. And only a movie could, he wrote, "destroy a movie, or, as in this case, several thousand war movies." Lester and Lennon, he wrote, "wrecked the war movie business by catching

WWII without its pants on."[172] Schneck loved that the sacred cow of World War II, which was remembered rather fondly amongst many Americans in particular, was finally being more honestly remembered as a horror and tragedy, rather than the glorious high-water mark of the American empire.

In November 1967, *Ramparts* published a review of The Beatles' recently released *Sgt. Pepper's Lonely Hearts Club Band* contributed by Nat Hentoff, who was a staff writer at the *New Yorker*. He described the Beatles as an important barometer to western civilization. He likewise considered Bob Dylan, the Beatles, and the Rolling Stones to be among the best artists in the business—the aristocracy of the industry. "They're making fewer and fewer compromises with commercialism," he gushed. And there was "hardly anything

---

[172] Stephen Schneck, "John Lennon Murders World War II," *Ramparts Magazine*, October 1967, p. 32.

interesting happening outside this exclusive circle."[173]

In June 1969, *Ramparts* published an article titled "Rock For Sale" contributed by Michael Lydon, who was a frequent contributor the *New York Times* on the subject of rock music. "Since that wildly exciting spring of 1967," he wrote, "the spring of *Sgt. Pepper's Lonely Hearts Club Band*, of be-ins and love-ins and flower-power, of the discovery of psychedelia, hippies and 'doing your thing' — to all of which "New Rock," as it then began to be called, was inextricably bound — one basic fact had been consistently ignored: rock was a product created, distributed and controlled for the profit of American (and international) corporations.[174]

---

[173] Nat Hentoff, "I Read The News Today," *Ramparts Magazine*, November 1967, p. 12.

[174] Michael Lydon, "Rock For Sale," *Ramparts Magazine*, June 1969, p. 19.

He lamented the commercialization of rock music as a hedonistic, vapid, and hollow counterrevolutionary force that sold kids conformity and capitalism packaged as independence and rebellion. The bitterest irony was, he asserted, that the "rock revolution" hype had come close to fatally limiting the revolutionary potential that rock did actually contain. So effective had the rock industry been in encouraging the spirit of optimistic youth take-over that rock's truly hard political edge, its constant exploration of the varieties of youthful frustration, had been ignored and softened. Rock musicians, like their followers, had always been torn between the obvious pleasures that America represented and the price paid for them. Rock and roll was not, he lamented, revolutionary music because it had never really ever gotten beyond articulation of this paradox. But at least rock had, he noted, offered an honest appraisal of where its makers and listeners were, and that radical, if bitterly defeatist, honesty was a touchstone, a starting point. If the companies, as representatives of the corporate structure, could convince the rock world that their revolution was won or almost won, that the walls of the playground were crumbling, he warned, not only would the constituents of rock seal their fate by that fatal self-deception, but their music, one of the few things they actually did have going for them, would ultimately be "corrupted and truly emasculated."[175]

In April 1971, *Ramparts* published an essay titled "I Wanna Hold Your Head: John Lennon After the Fall" written by Andrew Kopkind. In 1967 *Revolver*, then in 1969 *Magical Mystery Tour*, and in 1970 *Abbey Road* were nominated for best album by the Grammy Awards. But by 1971 the Beatles had disbanded. The myth of the Beatles was, Kopkind wrote, "a seed-dream of the '60s."

---

[175] Ibid, p. 24.

From it grew the rock religion to which massed millions of congregants around the world. In most respects it was, Kopkind wrote, "a complete cult, with a pantheon of gods, demigods, angels, priests and sacrificial virgins installed to cater to the range of human passions and needs." It was, he elaborated, also (like religion) big business. In time, the roster of divinities grew long, "but the Beatles retained the central throne. They claimed that they had superseded the old superstar, Jesus Christ, and for their adherents they were right." Then, as gods will, they fell to jealous fighting amongst themselves and went their separate ways, with their divinity still more or less intact. In the months prior to the publication of Kopkind's article, John Lennon had, he explained, taken it upon himself to do what few gods could ever do: "divest himself of his divinity" by declaring that he did not believe in Beatles in a song titled "God" on his first post-Beatles album *John Lennon/Plastic Ono*

Band.[176] Kopkind praised Lennon's line "Keep you doped with religion and sex and TV And you think you're so clever and classless and free But you're still fucking peasants as far as I can see A working-class hero is something to be."[177]

What Lennon found out through the process of making his first solo album was, Kopkind argued, the necessity for demystification, the possibility for breaking through myths, and the inevitability of honesty. Lennon ended the album, Kopkind concluded, "where we all have to begin." He cited Lennon who wrote, "And so, dear friends, you just have to carry on." What that meant to Kopkind was that it was imperative to shatter all the gods without us and within, to transfer power from our heroes to our

---

[176] Andrew Kopkind, "I Wanna Hold Your Head: John Lennon After the Fall," *Ramparts Magazine*, April 1971, p. 19.

[177] Ibid, p. 56.

imagination, to free ourselves from the isolation of private existence in a mass audience. The essential issue, in Lennon's terms, was "isolation," and how it would need to be resolved through intensive struggle.[178]

In July 1971, *Ramparts* published an interview with Lennon conducted by Robin Blackburn, who was an editor of Britain's *New Left Review*, and Tariq Ali, who was an editor of *The Red Mole*, titled "Lennon: The Working-Class Hero Turns Red." Lennon said he felt an obligation ... to write a song that people would sing in the pub or on a demonstration," and that he wanted to dedicate his energy, talent, and fame to composing songs for the revolution.[179] Lennon likewise noted the potential of popular culture being a counterrevolutionary force. "I think only by making the workers aware of the really

---

[178] Ibid, p. 56.

[179] Robin Blackburn and Tariq Ali, "Lennon: The Working-Class Hero Turns Red," *Ramparts Magazine*, July 1971, p. 43.

unhappy position they are in, breaking the dream they are surrounded by," Lennon said, was the best hope for a genuine and lasting social revolution. "They think they are in a wonderful free-speaking country; they've got cars and tellies and they don't want to think there's anything more to life; they are prepared to let the bosses run them, to see their children fucked up in school," he explained to Blackburn. "They're dreaming someone else's dream, it's not even their own."[180] Lennon then explained that music should not be the bubblegum pop of the early Beatles, but revolutionary. The idea was, he asserted, "not to comfort people, not to make them feel better, but to make them feel worse, to constantly put before them the degradations and humiliations they go through to get what they call a living wage."[181]

---

[180] Ibid, p. 49.

[181] Ibid, p. 49.

Two years after Jack Nicholson starred in the quintessential 1960s counterculture rock and roll film *Easy Rider* (1969) *Ramparts* published a profile of him written by Jon Stewart titled "Jack Nicholson Looks East." Stewart descried Nicholson as spearheading the nascent independent film revolution that was eroding the old studio system cartel that had for so long ruled Hollywood. The counterculture, in short, was revolutionizing the movie industry (or so it seemed in the early 1970s).

In June 1973, *Ramparts* published a report contributed by Kopkind titled "Reggae: The Steady Rock of Black Jamaica." The David Bowie-Lou Reed "genderfuck idea," Kopkind wrote, which was so promising in its beginning was already being blown by hype into "fatuous fraudulence," which left reggae as the next exploitable number for American record labels.[182] He saw the evolution of reggae as following the trajectory of American folk music in terms of being co-opted by corporate America and changed into pop music cloaked as countercultural rock and roll. He was fearful that reggae would not be resilient enough to survive the commercialization of such a revolutionary brand of roots music because it was "too fragile, too vulnerable, too honest to withstand the massive assaults on its authenticity that the collective corporate shuck would mount."[183] Kopkind proved to be prescient, considering Bob Marley's music in particularly had become muzak, elevator music, and the soundtrack for neophyte stoners to smoke dope to all through the waning stages of the twentieth century.

Sticking it to the Man

---

[182] Andrew Kopkind, "Reggae: The Steady Rock of Black Jamaica," *Ramparts Magazine*, June 1973, p. 50.

[183] Ibid, p. 51.

Much like William Powell's the *Anarchist Cookbook* (1971), *Ramparts* often expressed a "stick it to the man" ethos. Take, for instance, the essay titled, "Mercenary Job Wanted" contributed by Ted Braden, whose resume included the following:

> master parachutist, 911 logged jumps including 695 freefalls; ex-lieutenant and ex-sergeant U.S. Army; operated in 4 countries in SE Asia and 2 in Africa; experienced in use of U.S. weapons, demolitions, sabotage, infiltration; specialty is training and directing "hunter-killer" teams; 23 months of jungle operations in and out of Vietnam. Willing to organize and/or direct insurgency or counterinsurgency teams, whichever is appropriate to non-CIA supported employer. References can be checked with U.S. Army, U.S. Special Forces, CIA, and 5 Commando (Congo). Other talents by confidential inquiry

only. Absolute loyalty guaranteed to highest bidder. Contact: Ted B. Braden, Box 711, 301 Broadway, San Francisco.[184]

Braden faced a quandary after leaving the CIA. He had been trained to perform a certain set of skills with he could be paid very well for as a mercenary. "There's a great need for people with my talents," he wrote, but "while the CIA feels no qualms about hiring and using mercenaries," he explained, "in the Congo they don't want American citizens joining the mercenaries." The Agency, Braden noted, "wants American mercenaries in their direct employ (such as those they used to train and direct those for the Bay of Pigs caper). "Secondly," he elaborated, "while nobody gets upset if a British or Rhodesian mercenary is killed, it would be embarrassing for the CIA if it became known that an American mercenary

---

[184] Ted B. Braden, "Mercenary Job Wanted," *Ramparts Magazine*, October 1967, p. 22.

was killed or captured. They always prefer to work through other nationals. I need work and I don't mean driving somebody's truck."[185]

The fact that *Ramparts* published Braden's plea for someone to hire him was a kind of thumb in the eye that seemed to illuminate that the CIA had let a genie out of the bottle, in this case a brazen and seemingly anti-ideological and apolitical pure capitalist mercenary for hire. He concluded by stating his particular desire to get back to the Congo but feared the state department would prevent him. "Too bad," he lamented, "because the anti-Mobutu boys are making a bundle."[186] Braden's conclusion also seemed to also indicate that the publishers of *Ramparts* were openly advocating Braden's eagerness to fight against Joseph Mobutu's forces in Congo, which were heavily armed by the CIA.

---

[185] Ibid, p. 22.

[186] Ibid, p. 26.

Ramparts somewhat odd decision to publish Braden's resume and essay was, like numerous pranks and performances concocted by the Yippies, unnecessarily brazen and antagonistic to the CIA and state department, which *Ramparts* consistently depicted to be forces of tyranny around the globe. It was therefore perhaps unwise to conspicuously define the magazine as the muckraking anti-thesis and avowed enemy of entities that it also depicted to be incredibly sinister and powerful. As valuable and necessary as *Ramparts'* muckraking was during the life of the magazine, the kind of arrogant chicanery evident in the editors publication of "Mercenary Job Wanted" seemed to be the editors engaging in a kind of metaphorical and quite childish self-immolation that could undermine the very causes the magazine had so consistently championed as a mouthpiece of the New Left. The editors in some sense abandoned the moral high ground they had sought to cultivate in contrast to the CIA by publishing Braden's essay. It also foreshadowed the increased militancy happening in the U.S. and around the globe in 1967, especially in the wake of the assassination of Che Guevara, and the disintegration in 1969 of the New Left into two camps: those advocating violence versus those who perceived violence to be self-defeating.

In September 1967, *Ramparts* published an essay titled "The Case for Bugging" contributed by private eye Hal Lipset that provided a tutorial on how to tap a phone. The article was a kind of tongue-in-cheek critique of the FBI's illegal penchant for spying on American citizens, especially activist liberals such as Martin Luther King, Jr.

In August 1970, *Ramparts* published an editorial titled "The San Francisco Mime Troupe: Ripping Off Ma Bell." The Troupe's newest play targeted The (Bell) Telephone Company. Public opinion polls indicated that the general popularity of the phone company was somewhat less than that of the parking-meter industry. The Troupe's play subversively described a method for making do-it-yourself telephone credit cards for use on station-to-station calls from phone booths. The phone company evidently surmised that this knowledge about their credit cards might be used to deny the company the rightful fruits of initiative, competence and financial risks. They thus hit the Mime Troupe for a couple of hundred dollars on somebody else's unauthorized credit card calls; they even threatened to remove the phone from their playhouse. The editorial concluded by informing readers that The Mime Troupe was available for bookings in the Bay Area during the summer, and elsewhere during the winter and provided their contact information, joking "no credit card calls accepted.[187]

---

[187] *Ramparts* editorial staff, "The San Francisco Mime Troupe: Ripping Off Ma Bell," *Ramparts Magazine*, August 1970, p. 26.

In February 1971, *Ramparts* published an article titled "America on $0 a Day" contributed by Abbie Hoffman, who was a co-founder of the Youth International Party (the Yippies). His essay provided a guide for how to live freely for free. He explained the best way to rip-off restaurants and supermarkets in addition to taking advantage of free food programs in American cities. He also explained ways of getting "free money" by collecting welfare and/or unemployment benefits. "It's so easy to get on welfare," Hoffman wrote, "that anyone who is broke and doesn't have a regular relief check coming in is nothing but a goddam lazy bum."[188] He, like the San Francisco Mine Troupe, informed readers about the free phone calls waiting for those with the knowhow to rip-off Ma Bell. He also celebrated the free pets available at shelters and the fact that every year the National Park

---

[188] Abbie Hoffman, "America on $0 a Day," *Ramparts Magazine*, February 1971, p. 51.

Service gave away surplus elk in order to keep the herds under its jurisdiction from outgrowing the amount of available land for grazing. He provided a mailing address for Superintendent at Yellowstone National Park, in Wyoming. It was safe to assume that the whole elk part of the story was a gag on readers and the Superintendent who was likely inundated by letters from gullible hippies with a hankering for an elk or two. Hoffman also sardonically noted that for those interested in "free atrocities" that the Army had a surplus available. For those in need of free toilets, he urged them to "SNEAK UNDER!"[189] As lighthearted and humorous as Hoffman's tutorial on how to live free for free in America was, it was also deleterious in the sense that it added fodder to conservatives such as Ronald Reagan who bemoaned that the welfare system was rife with corruption and inspired chiselers

---

[189] Ibid, p. 55.

of the system. In other words, in his eagerness to put his thumb in the eye of the likes of Richard Nixon and Ronald Reagan he in fact made it more difficult for the poor folks he professed to represent to get the help they desperately needed to survive.

In April 1972, *Ramparts* published a tutorial titled "How to Cheat on Your Income Tax: A Guide" contributed by "Bob Cratchit," which was the pseudonym of an accountant that was serving a 2 to 10 year bid at Soledad Prison in California for embezzlement, not tax evasion. He argued that when the dust on the soon-to-be conclusion of the tax season settled the most prominent among the winners would be a couple hundred millionaires and a few thousand corporations — none of which would pay a penny in taxes. They got off scot-free, Cratchit explained, because their accountants understood accelerated depreciation, investment credits, depletion allowances and carryforward/carrybacks. Such devices in effect constituted an independent set of rules which, "when manipulated by the pink and silken hand of the corporate tax accountant," delivered untold tax savings. As for the losers (the vast majority of American taxpayers), they paid for this corporate welfare and increasingly blamed welfare recipients rather than the "winners" which Cratchit described above. His advice was to simply lie and take the chances that the IRS would not catch them or spare the expense to prosecute a small time tax chiseler. "While I am convinced that my IRS agent informer is right," he wrote, "that criminal fraud charges are just never brought against petty tax chiselers, I am even more sure that, even if the feds do come after you, they cannot prove a thing." The only way for the IRS to prove fraud would be, he explained, to admit to it, which he had unfortunately learned the hard way. In other words, commit fraud, and if caught, simply lie or plead their fifth amendment right and they would be in the clear. Cratchit's article, like Hoffman's was humorous, but actually quite irresponsible and potentially destructive towards leftists causes such as tax reform and salutary to conservatives aiming to depict liberals as liars, lazy, criminal, chiselers, and cheats. These kinds of articles about committing fraud are couched in a humorous "we're sticking it to the man" vibe. But it actually likely undermined the New Left's claim to moral authority for many readers and quite likely more self-destructive than helpful a movement already coming apart.

The theme of sticking-it-to-the man was, however, pushed against in the June 1972 edition of *Ramparts* in a three-part series titled "Food [Stamp] Conspiracy: No. That's Bankrupt Hippie Morality." The first in the series was contributed by Sheldon Heuchler, who rightly wrote that, "ripping off' food stamps did not hurt the system; it hurt the poor. The reason, he noted, was simple: there

374

was not an unlimited amount of money around. The welfare supervisors who might have been worried that too many people were getting welfare, would often find it easier to reject the poor, inarticulate welfare applicant than tangle with the well-educated dropout. Most people on welfare and food stamps, he explained, were not simply loafers—"they couldn't get a job if they tried."[190] Being a welfare hustler thus, he warned, was quite different from being a revolutionary, and the rip-off mentality was "much closer to crime than to social change." When people said that their very existence was revolutionary, that their pilgrimage to self-indulgence and good vibes was itself their social contribution, they fooled no one, he wrote. The left would do well to dissociate itself from these people, he warned, and to "discriminate sharply between

---

[190] Sheldon Heuchler, "Food [Stamp] Conspiracy: No. That's Bankrupt Hippie Morality," *Ramparts Magazine*, June 1972, p. 14.

those who can't find work and those who consciously and joyously are freeloading, and urge the latter to leave food stamps for those who really need them.[191]

Heuchler's argument was rejoined in the June 1972 edition or *Ramparts* by another piece contributed by "Bob Cratchit" to the "Food [Stamp] Conspiracy" series titled "Go Ahead, The Best Things in Life Are Free." He sardonically quipped to Heuchler, "we are off to join the working class, just like daddy did back in '32. And, now that you are working, you turn on the hippies who aren't."[192] In other words, Cratchit indicated that Heuchler's arguments presented in the essay mentioned above cast him into the role of the proverbial "man." Heuchler, Cratchit argued, took his notion that there was only so much money to go around as being derived from an economic

---

[191] Ibid, p. 63.
[192] "Bob Cratchit," "Go Ahead. The Best Things in Life Are Free," *Ramparts Magazine*, June 1972, p. 15.

logic popularized in the nineteenth century, succumbing to a version of the vicious "wages fund" doctrine. Pre-Keynesian economists held that only a fixed amount of money was available for workers and that any attempt to raise wage rates would only serve to slice up the pie into a smaller number of larger pieces, putting some out of work so that others may prosper. "A useful theory for the employer no doubt," Cratchit wrote, "but hardly consistent with modern economics." The fallacy was, he asserted, obvious: "first of all," he noted, "this is not a barnyard cooperative nor a socialistic society where my laziness requires my neighbors toil." As such, he explained, it made no difference whether or not he worked, or prospered, or for that matter, starved. A system called capitalism, he explained, acted as a contraceptive on American's economic interdependency. Hippie ethics were thus, he informed Heuchler, "subversive," while "work ethics" were "supportive of the present system." He, however, conceded that Heuchler was right when he wrote that the newly popular rip-off ethos angered the dominant powers, whose retaliation lead to anti-welfare rebellion, tax protest, and even worse their usual hassling of the deserving poor. "That is true and it's bad," Cratchit conceded. "But why are we to be held responsible for the irrationality of others?" he rhetorically asked.[193] What Cratchit failed to understand, it would however seem, was that welfare was part of actual budget that was indeed finite, which further bolstered conservatives attacks on welfare recipients as fraudulent chiselers who were simply too lazy to get a job and were thus ripping off the average working American, which drove a wedge between the working poor who increasingly voted Republican in the waning decades of the twentieth century and those who were unable

---

[193] Ibid, p. 15.

to find gainful employment due in part to an educational system that had failed them.

The third contribution to the "Food [Stamp] Conspiracy" series published in June 1972 was an editorial titled "How to Get Them." The editors noted that Democratic Senator from the state of Florida, Spessard Holland, had recently announced to his colleagues the newly agreed-upon gimmick to stop hippies from chiseling welfare. Holland decided to redefine the term "household" to exclude households consisting of unrelated individuals under the age of sixty, such as hippie communes. Welfare guidelines varied from state to state depending on the political situation and the strength of local food stamp conspiracies. For example, welfare was hardest to get in Governor Reagan's California. The editors thus urged readers to check with their local office of the National Welfare Rights Organization. The essay was essentially a tutorial for communards to strategically get around the so called "household" definition gimmick Holland proposed, which included one hippie adopting another hippie and intentionally doing poorly in job interviews in order to continue to receive unemployment benefits.

The attention turned back to ripping off phone companies in the back pages of the June 1972 edition of *Ramparts* in an essay written by an anonymous contributor who referred to his/herself as "R. Oklahoma." The essay was titled "Regulating the Phone Company in Your Home." It had, Oklahoma wrote, generally been assumed that the free long distance phone call was accessible only to those able to build a "Blue Box," an electronic device that generated the in-band signaling audio tones that used to be used to control long-distance telephone exchanges. By generating the same tones employed by a telephone operator's dialing console, a Blue Box user could route their own calls and bypass the normal toll collection used by the telephone company. Oklahoma's essay demonstrated how practically anyone who could change the plug on an electric toaster — using only a screwdriver, a kitchen knife, and four dollars' worth of readily available electric parts — could build in two to three hours a simple device capable of evading charges on long distance telephone calls. This was not the Blue Box, which enabled the user to make long distance calls for free, but a version of the Mute Box, which enabled the user to receive them free of charge. Oklahoma than provided tips on how to evade being detected by the phone company, including keeping class short so that the company could not hone in the signal.

A month after *Ramparts* published "Regulating the Phone Company in Your Home" the editors published a story titled "Suppression: How the Phone Company Interrupted Our Service." In June 1972 the editors had unwittingly violated a little known law that made it illegal to sell "plans or instructions" for any "instrument, apparatus or device" intended to avoid telephone toll charges, and that the penalty for violation was up-to-a-year in jail.[194] Within a week of the publication of "Regulating the Phone Company in Your Home" American Telephone and Telegraph had achieved what the CIA, Pentagon, FBI and other targets of *Ramparts'* muckraking journalism over the previous ten years had not been able to bring about: the nationwide suppression of the magazine. It was, the editors lamented, no surprise that AT&T did not look on constitutional protections such as freedom of the press as serious constraints. "For the company's entire corporate experience was that the structure of law and government served as instruments of its power, to be recklessly manipulated for advantage." AT&T was, after all, first among giants, the largest American corporation of any

---

[194] California Penal Code, section 502.7.

kind, with an incredible $45 billion in assets and a net income larger than the total for the nation's fifty largest commercial banks or the fifty largest retail firms combined. Its closest point of contact with the rule of law was in the context of utility regulation, where only the facade of serious independent authority was still maintained.[195] The loss of revenue from the June edition pulled from shelves promised to pose serious consequences for the magazine's survival and the publication was thus suing W.A. Krueger, the printing company that surreptitiously gave over proprietary information to AT&T, which in turn sued the Bell System for damages. "We are," the editors declared, "further establishing a war chest to regulate AT&T journalistically by revealing the ways in which it cheats and

---

[195] *Ramparts* editorial staff, "How the Phone Company Interrupted Our Service," *Ramparts Magazine*, July 1972, p. 11.

defrauds the captive customers" who are forced to rely on its monopolistic systems.[196]

In October 1972, *Ramparts* published an essay titled "Phone Phreak-Out in Phun City" contributed by Robert Sherman. On July 29, 1972, Sherman wrote, the basement ballroom of the Hotel Diplomat in New York City was the site of a convention of hackers eager to get revenge on Ma Bell for what they had done to *Ramparts*. This was the First International Phone Phreak Convention, sponsored by the Youth International Party Line. Originally scheduled in Miami during the Democratic Convention, it was postponed and moved to Manhattan where, Yippies said, the laws against phreaking were "full of loopholes."[197] Although the Yippies had failed to deliver on their pledge to have phone calls from phone phreaks the world over, a

---

[196] Ibid, p. 11.
[197] Robert Sherman, "Phone Phreak-Out in Phun City," *Ramparts Magazine*, October 1972, p. 12.

wonderful time was had by all — all, that was, except for Ma Bell's Special Agents, who attended the convention at the invitation of The Party Line.[198]

Conclusion

As the above articles might illuminate, there was a great deal of dissonance in the counterculture and the New Left over the issue of ethics and ideals. At a moment when conservatives were finding common cause on wedge issues such as *Roe v. Wade* and a perceived lack of law and order the counterculture was ripping itself apart. *Ramparts* published a few articles that touched on the unraveling of the counterculture and retreat of members of the New Left from the realm of politics and into new ageism. In July 1973, for example, *Ramparts* published an article titled "A Reader's Guide to the New Mysticism" contributed "Joshu," which

---

[198] Ibid, p. 13.

provided definitions and/or explications for terms that still might have been quite foreign to Americans in the mid-1970s, including Ananda Marg, Arica, Divine Light Mission, EST, The Foundation, Mind Control, Sufism, Tibetan Buddhism, and Zen.[199]

"A Reader's Guide to the New Mysticism" was followed in the July 1973 edition of *Ramparts* by an investigative report titled "Blissed Out With The Perfect Master" contributed by Ken Kelley, who was a managing editor of the *Berkeley Barb*. He wrote a less than favorable account of Rennie Davis' newfound devotion to Satguru Maharaj Ji – "the teenage theomorphic guru" from India.[200] Davis, the former member of the infamous May Day Tribe, was returning to Berkeley for the first time since standing trial for conspiracy

---

[199] Joshu, "A Reader's Guide to the New Mysticism," *Ramparts Magazine*, July 1973, pp. 30-31.

[200] Ken Kelley, "Blissed Out With The Perfect Master," *Ramparts Magazine*, July 1973, p. 32.

to incite a riot at the 1968 Democratic National Convention in Chicago. Some eight years earlier, Mario Savio and his fellow students had marched to shut down the University of California, thereby unloosing a flood of campus protests which did not subside for five years. Davis had also played a crucial role in that movement. Now, Kelley bemoaned, he was "telling us to surrender our hearts and minds to a barely pubescent self-proclaimed Perfect Master from India and waltz into Nirvana." It was, Kelley lamented, "as if Che Guevara had returned to recruit for the Campfire Girls: the anomaly was as profound as the amazement."[201] Davis explained that The Divine Light Mission and he were, despite critics that believed he had abandoned actually the New Left, was at the forefront of the revolution. There were no sexual hang-ups in the Divine Light Mission because there was no sex, and the group planned to eventually

---

[201] Ibid, p. 32.

eliminate distinctions between men and women altogether. It was, Kelley concluded, the ultimate irony of the movement's search for answers that there were none -- only more questions, more struggle which grew ever more difficult as the questions became ever harder to ask.

The counterculture initially represented revolution of American society. It was, however, quickly co-opted by advertising agents eager to sell products to kids. As such, many of the adherents of the counterculture increasingly fled the mainstream culture altogether, opting instead to live on communes removed from the mainstream and/or explore new ageism as a means and method of self-revolution, thereby abandoning what many increasingly perceived to be a futile struggle against a materialistic and militarist society, thereby championing the notion that revolution would not be overt nor through revolutionizing American institutions, but by enough people revolutionizing their own spiritual mindset and existence. In hindsight, this social revolution via individuals checking out from the mainstream of the American polity never materialized. And though the counterculture represented the hope and promise of a kinder, gentler, more egalitarian society, it was, like so many other aspects of the rights revolution that *Ramparts* often eloquently narrated rolled systemically back in the waning decades of the twentieth century, especially after the end of the Cold War as what was once known as the Third World was opened to economic development and exploitation.

EPILOGUE

From 1962 - 1975 *Ramparts Magazine* the efforts of traditionally marginalized Americans demanding civil rights and social equality. The magazine focused specifically on efforts made by Mexican Americans, Native Americans, and

African Americans to attain economic and political equality. The magazine also championed the Women's Liberation Movement, and ardently supported the notion that all Americans had a right to adequate and affordable healthcare. *Ramparts* also, as the pages above illuminate, advocated the rise of the Modern Environmentalist Movement, subsequent to chronicling the growing prominence of what came to be known as the counterculture in American society during the 1960s and 1970s.

www.ingramcontent.com/pod-product-compliance
Lightning Source LLC
Chambersburg PA
CBHW030517230426
43665CB00010B/653